Dinosaur

Learn About Dinosaurs and Enjoy Colorful Pictures

(Learn the Fun Facts You've Always Wanted to Know About Dinosaurs)

Carrie Theriot

Published By **Oliver Leish**

Carrie Theriot

Dinosaur: Learn About Dinosaurs and Enjoy Colorful Pictures (Learn the Fun Facts You've Always Wanted to Know About Dinosaurs)

ISBN 978-1-77485-755-7

Legal & Disclaimer

The information contained in this ebook is not designed to replace or take the place of any form of medicine or professional medical advice. The information in this ebook has been provided for educational & entertainment purposes only.

The information contained in this book has been compiled from sources deemed reliable, and it is accurate to the best of the Author's knowledge; however, the Author cannot guarantee its accuracy and validity and cannot be held liable for any errors or omissions. Changes are periodically made to this book. You must consult your doctor or get professional medical advice before using any of the suggested remedies, techniques, or information in this book.

Upon using the information contained in this book, you agree to hold harmless the Author from and against any damages, costs, and expenses, including any legal fees potentially resulting from the application of any of the

TABLE OF CONTENTS

Chapter 1: Prior To The Triassic Period

The dinosaurs lived for a long time ago. It was within the Mesozoic Era, which covers the time period that spans between 252 million years and 65 millennia ago.

The Mesozoic Era can be subdivided into three distinct periods:

*The Triassic Period from 252 million years ago to 200 million years ago.

*The Jurassic Period from 201 million years ago to the age of 145 millions of years ago.

*The Cretaceous Period from 145 million years ago to 66 million years ago.

The dinosaur world was quite different from the world of the present. Diverse dinosaurs and other species were present at different times during the Mesozoic Era. The Mesozoic Era lasted for a long duration. In actual fact, the time between the first dinosaurs ' appearance and the final non-avian (non-bird) dinosaurs dying out is significantly more than that been passed since dinosaurs went extinct.

The book we'll concentrate on the first of three geological periods of the Mesozoic that is known as the Triassic Period. Dinosaurs & Other

Animals of the Jurassic and Dinosaurs & Other Animals of the Cretaceous.

The Mesozoic Era could seem to be an eternity ago however, you should know that the Earth is much, much older... Scientists have concluded that the Earth is around 4550 millions of years old. There is more information about the beginning of Earth by reading my work Before the Dinosaurs, but for now , let's briefly go over the major instances.

Earth's Formation Formation of the Solar System and Earth

Researchers believe scientists believe that the Solar System was formed about 4600 million years ago, from a massive cloud of gas and dust called a molecular cloud. It is believed that a nearby explosion star (a supernova) could have disturbed the molecular cloud and created the region with a significant amount of matter (known as an nebula that was pre-solar).

Particles that were part of the cloud were attracted by one another through gravity's pull. The elements eventually formed an object, known as protoplanetary disk. When the protoplanetary disk got larger and more dense it began spinning. The denser and smaller the disk got the more rapidly it turned.

Protoplanetary disk:

The Sun is a large gas ball, was is formed in the middle of the disk, where there were the largest amount of particles. The heat that was released by collisions between particles as well as the density of the particles ultimately allowed the Sun to attain nuclear the process of fusion. It is the method that allows the Sun produces energy today when hydrogen atoms are fused together to create Helium Atoms.

The Sun:

In the outer regions of the disc, particles slowly became one through a process called the process of accretion. There were initially small grains however, they gradually grew into clumps that were around 200 metres (650 feet) in the diameter. The clumps collided with one creating larger, larger bodies. These are known as planetesimals by scientists and measured around 10-kilometers (6.2 miles) in size. The planetesimals slowly hit one another to create bigger and more massive bodies. After numerous collisions, the bodies eventually evolved into planets, which includes our home planet, Earth.

Researchers believe the Earth as well as the Moon were created by a Mars-sized object colliding into the proto-Earth

You can learn further about the Sun and the planets as well as the history of the Solar System in my book, The Solar System.

The Hadean Eon

The most ancient period of Earth's history is called The Hadean Eon (also known as the Pre-Archean Eon). It is the Hadean Eon spans the period that began the creation of the Earth 4550 million years ago, to 4 million years long ago.

Very few rocks remain from The Hadean Eon and relatively little is known about the Earth during this time. Up until recently, the general consensus of scientists was that the planet's surface was mostly molten, and the conditions in the Earth were so unhospitable that there was any life. Recently , however certain experts have been questioning this consensus and suggest possible liquid-water sources, and possibly the possibility of primitive forms of life.

Artist's vision of Earth in the Hadean Eon:

The Archean Eon

The following period following that of the Hadean Eon is called the Archean Eon (also spelled Archaean Eon or Archaean Eon). This Archean Eon spans the period between 4000 million years ago and the 2,500 million year ago.

In the Archean the period of liquid water was plentiful and the first lifeform, simply one-celled (unicellular) organisms, known as prokaryota, developed. Prokaryota remain in existence to this day, and are divided into two groups:

* Archaea (singular: archeon)

* Bacteria (singular: bacterium)

The earliest forms of life could be found in hydrothermal vents that were located in the oceans:

The Proterozoic Eon

The time period following that Archean Eon is called the Proterozoic Eon. The Proterozoic Eon was a time period between two million years ago to 541 million year ago. In the first half of the Proterozoic multicellular organisms that were more sophisticated and complex called the eukaryota appeared. Similar to prokaryota, eurkaryota with single cells exist today however, towards the end of Proterozoic the eurkaryota began to coexist in groups, the first multicellular organisms.

Fossil from one of early multicellular species (from the Ediacaran Period of the Proterozoic) is on display at Houston Museum of Natural Science. Houston Museum of Natural Science:

The Phanerozoic Eon

The Phanerozoic Eon is the period where multicellular life first emerged and then spread to the entire planet. It spans from 541 million years prior to today. It is divided into three periods of geology:

*The Paleozoic Era (also spelled Palaeozoic Era) between 541 million years ago and 252 million years ago.

*The Mesozoic Era, which occurred between 252 million years and 66 million years ago.

*The Cenozoic Era, which spanned the 66 million year mark to the present.

The era in question is divided into times:

*The Paleozoic Era is subdivided into the Cambrian Period, the Ordovician Period The Silurian Period, the Devonian Period as well as The Carboniferous Period (sometimes subdivided into the Mississippian Subperiod and Pennsylvanian Subperiod) and the Permian Period.

*The Mesozoic Era is divided into three parts: the Triassic Period, the Jurassic Period and the Cretaceous Period.

*The Cenozoic Era is divided into three parts: the Paleogene Period (also spelled Palaeogene Period or Palaeogene Period), the Neogene Period and the Quaternary Period.

The Paleozoic Era

In the early Paleozoic in the Paleozoic period, a myriad of new kinds of multicellular living appeared abruptly in an event referred to as the Cambrian explosion. The new species were first discovered in the oceans and included members of the familiar group of animals, such as chordates (animals that have a spinal cord like vertebrates) arthropods (the category that includes spiders, insects, crustaceans and so on.) and Mollusks.

Trilobites, among the most effective early multicellular creatures, initially emerged within the Cambrian Period:

As the Paleozoic advanced, life slowly spread across the earth. Forests and plants flourished across every continent, and were closely followed by animals, such as arthropods and then the tetrapods (vertebrates with four legs).

Edaphosaurus lived in the latter portion of Paleozoic Era, the Permian Period:

The end of the Paleozoic Era

The end of the Paleozoic there was a major event that took place. The mass extinction, which was the most devastating ever recorded in the history of Earth and is referred to as the Permian Triassic Extinction Event (also called the P-Tr Extinction, the P-T Extinction or The End-Permian Extinction, and the Great Dying). This , along with the other mass extinctions that took place throughout the Triassic are covered in greater detail in Chapter 10.

More than 90 to 95 percent of marine species and about 70 percent of terrestrial species perished in the Permian-Triassic extinctions. This meant that when the next period of geological time called known as the Triassic Period (which is the beginning that is part of the Mesozoic Era) there were numerous vacant ecological niches, as well as numerous opportunities for the introduction of new species. This period, called the Triassic Period, which is the primary topic of this book.

Chapter 2: Introduction To The Triassic Period

The Triassic Period was named by German geologist Friedrich August von Alberti (September 4th, 1795 until September 12th 1878) in 1834. Alberti acknowledged that fossils found in 3 distinct layers (strata) located in northern Europe all referred to a single time period in the history of geology on Earth. The three layers were named "Trias" due to the Latin word trias , which translates to triad, so the period of geological evidence is known as"The Triassic Period." Triassic Period.

Friedrich August von Alberti:

As per the current naming conventions The Triassic Period is the first of three periods in the Mesozoic Era. The Triassic is the period that runs from 252 million years ago until 200 million years ago.

The start and the end of the Triassic Period was marked by two massive mass extinctions

* The Triassic started immediately following the biggest mass extinction of Earth's history, called the Permian-Triassic extinct event. The planet was devastated by various species of plants and animals being destroyed. The survivors were able to inherit the Earth and developed into a range of new life forms which included early dinosaurs.

9

* The Triassic ended with a different mass extinction. However, it was not as devastating as the Permian-Triassic extinct. This mass extinction is also known as the Triassic-Jurassic extinction. Like other mass extinctions Triassic-Jurassic extermination wiped out a variety of kinds of species of plants and animals and created opportunities for survivors to survive the next geological time, in this case, it being the Jurassic Period.

* The Permian-Triassic extinction and the Triassic-Jurassic extinction and the mass extinctions that took place in the Triassic are further explored in chapter 10.

Subdivisions (Epochs) of the Triassic Period

It is believed that the Triassic Period is subdivided into three Epochs (also called series) each further divided into three or two age groups. The Epochs include:

* Early Triassic - The Early Triassic (also called"the Lower Triassic or the Scythian) corresponds to 4 million years in the beginning in the Triassic Period. This period was between approximately 250 million years old and 247 million year ago.

* Middle Triassic - The Middle Triassic (sometimes abbreviated to Tr2) is the following

10-million years within the Triassic Period. This is the period between 247 million year ago to 237 million.

* Late Triassic - The Late Triassic (sometimes called The Upper Triassic or Tr3) is longer than the other three times being roughly 36 million years in length. This is the period between approximately 237 million year ago and 201 million years ago.

Early Triassic Epoch

The Early Triassic is the epoch that followed the Permian Triassic extinct. Many species were eliminated by the mass extinction including all trilobites that remain, along with a myriad of species of brachiopods and ammonoids corals and the echinoderms (starfish as well as brittle stars, sea urchins, and their closely related) Mollusks, and other marine invertebrates. On land, the majority of huge species had gone extinct. After the mass extinction the most commonly encountered terrestrial animal is Lystrosaurus that was a small herbivore dizynodont (a similar reptile to a mammal) with two teeth that resembled tusks.

Lystrosaurus skeleton:

The animals that survived extinctions faced a brutal world. Although it's certain that many ecological niches were empty however, the plant life had not completely recovered. The climate was also very hot as a result of global warming caused by carbon dioxide emissions by recent eruptions of volcanoes (see chapter 4). The landmasses of Earth were joined into the supercontinent of immense size (see Chapter 3) with vast inland areas which were mostly covered by deserts. The only areas of temperate climate were areas near the poles.

Three million years after 3 million years into the Early Triassic, around 249 million years ago, a second catastrophe occurred. It is referred to as the Smith-Spathian event and is believed to be due to rising temperatures. When temperatures in the tropical regions of the sea were at 40 degrees Celsius (104degF) Large and mobile animals were eliminated from these regions as well as a number of smaller, immobile species perished out. Animals and plants returned to the tropics 2 million years on, approximately 247 million years back at which point temperatures dropped back to normal levels.

Scientists have only recently acknowledged it was the case that Smith-Spathian is an extinct event. This is due to the fact that a lot of species were already dying in the Permian-

Triassic extinction , that the evidence for loss of species in the Smith-Spathian is extremely limited. However, the study of the fossils from conodonts (extinct toothless jawless fish that resembles Eels) as well as the loss of half the bivalve mollusk species found in the tropics, prove the existence of this event of extinction.

Conodonts are jawless fish that have gone extinct, and they're known mostly for their tooth-like fossils (microfossils):

Scientists have subdivided this Early Triassic into two ages (also called stages):

*The Induan Age - The Induan Age is the earliest phase of Early Triassic, lasted about 700,000 years and took place from 252 million to 251 million years between 252 million between 251 million and the 251 million year ago. Since the Induan starts immediately after the Triassic-Permian extinction There were a few species of animals, and biodiversity was very low throughout the globe as a whole , and within specific geographic regions. Furthermore, the oceans as well as numerous freshwater areas are anoxic (low levels of oxygen) which made living difficult in these areas.

*The Olenekian Age - The Olenekian Age is the final stage of Early Triassic, lasted about 4 million years. It was observed sometime between the 251 million year mark between 247 billion years prior. The Olenekian is often separated into Smithian subage (or Smithian substage) and Spathian subage (or Spathian substage). The conditions were not easy, however new groups were discovered, including species of reptiles, mammal-like reptiles. The first Ichthyopterygians (reptiles with flippers which are similar to dolphins) as well as early modern amphibians (lissamphibians). The Smith-Spathian extinction event took place during the Olenekian.

Proterosuchus was reptile that lived through The Late Induan Age and through the Olenekian Age:

Middle Triassic Epoch

The Middle Triassic is the second period that was part of the Triassic Period and spans the interval between 247 million prior to 237 million ago. In older works it is said that the Middle Triassic is sometimes referred to as Muschelkalk however nowadays, this term is used to describe the sedimentary rock strata that occurred during the period that occurred in western and central Europe.

The Middle Triassic is characterized by the ongoing revival of life following the Permian

Triassic extinction, which includes the finalization of the restoration of woody trees. The vertebrates which first appeared in the Middle Triassic are various types of marine reptiles (see Chapter 6) as well as archosaurs and their closest cousins (see Chapter 7) and early dinosaurs (see Chapter 8).).

Fossil of the Crinoid Encrinus Liiiformis of the Middle Triassic:

Scientists divide into the Middle Triassic into two ages:

*The Anisian Age - The Anisian Age is the earlier portion of Middle Triassic. It spans from 247 million years back between 247 million and 242 million years ago.

*The Ladinian Age - The Ladinian Age is the most recent portion of Middle Triassic. It covers the period that was between the 242 million year ago and 237 million years ago.

Fossil from Ceratites evolutus, an ammonoid from the beginning of the Triassic (Anisian Age) of the Middle Triassic:

Fossil from the fish Archaeosemionotus , from the latter part (Ladinian Age) of the Middle Triassic:

Late Triassic Epoch

The Late Triassic is the third and final epoch in the Triassic Period. It spans that was between 237 and the year 201 million.

Numerous new species of dinosaurs were discovered in The Late Triassic. The other new species to evolve include Pterosaurs (flying reptiles) and early turtles the very first Lepidosauromorpha (the reptile group that includes snakes, lizards as well as tuataras, and their cousins) and the early ancestors of the first mammals.

Proganochelys is the oldest-known turtle with a fully-shelled shell:

Scientists divide this Late Triassic into three ages:

*The Carnian Age - The Carnian Age corresponds to the first portion of Late Triassic. It spans that was between 237 millions years ago between 227 million and 227 million years ago.

*The Norian Age - The Norian Age is a middle of Late Triassic. It spans from 227 million years back up to 208.5 million years ago.

*The Rhaetian Age - The Rhaetian Age is the final portion of Late Triassic. It spans between 208.5 million years between the era of 201 million years in the past. The mass extinct (the

Triassic-Jurassic extinction) was observed during this time but it's not certain if it was a sudden event or a gradual event that lasted for many million years. The Triassic-Jurassic extinctions wiped out between 76 percent to 83% marine and terrestrial species. In addition to all conodonts, it especially affected ammonoids and bivalve gastropods, brachiopods as well as marine reptiles. It appears, however, to have minimal impact on other groups, like crocodiles, fish, cynodonts , and pterosaurs. The issue of extinction is explored more in Chapter 10.

Fossil Araucaria tree trunk dating to the late Triassic Epoch

Chapter 3: Pale Geography And The Triassic Period

If you are standing in the earth, one could feel as if the Earth is solid under your feet. While it's real that the exterior layer is solid, the interior of the Earth is solid, below it is a complicated system of layers that includes melting rocks (the Earth's interior is described in greater details in Chapter 5 in the book I wrote, The Solar System).

The outer crust of the solid layer of Earth is generally five to 10km (3 up to six miles) deep in the oceanic regions as well as 30-50 km (20 up to 30 miles) thick in continental regions. Additionally, the exterior crust has been divided in plates that are floating on top of a layer fluid (molten) rock referred to as the mantle. For very long time periods the plates may slow-moving around. Normal movement is between 10 and 40 millimeters (0.4 to 1.6 inches) annually, however "fast" movements can exceed 163 millimeters (6.3 inches) each year. The motion of the plates in the crust cause the landmasses of Earth to shift in a slow manner (continental drift). The entire process is referred to as plate tectonics.

The positions of continents and landmasses of the Earth have changed over the course of millions of years The globe didn't always look the way it is now. Studying the geography of geological past is referred to as paleogeography.

The positions of the continents prior to that of the Triassic within the Late Permian, and during the Triassic:

Scientists believe that during the Late Permian and at the beginning of the Triassic Period, all the major landmasses of the world were united into one huge supercontinent. The supercontinent is referred to as Pangaea (also called Pangea) that means "all the earth". Pangaea extended from the far north, nearly reaching beyond the North pole, all the way to the equator, all up to beyond the South the pole, and even further. The most notable aspect of Pangaea's geology was the presence of a sea that cut through the supercontinent from east, along the equator. This was identified as"the Tethys Ocean (also called Tethys Sea (also known as Tethys Sea or The Neotethys). The supercontinent was surrounded by a huge ocean, called by scientists Panthalassa meaning "all of the ocean".

When it was the Triassic Period progressed, Pangaea began to split. A different sea began to separate the northern portion of Pangaea (called Laurasia) from the southern portion (called Gondwanaland or Gondwana).

One of the consequences of all the earth's landmasses becoming one is that there were only a few coastal areas that were near shore shallow water One supercontinent has a much smaller shoreline than smaller continents. This is why Triassic sedimentary deposits in the marine environment are uncommon, though they are abundant in the west of Europe which is where the first study to understand the Triassic was conducted. But, we don't know anything about the existence of Panthalassa in the Triassic due to the fact that plates of the ocean are constantly being recycled back into the earth's inner core (subduction) in addition to the fact that there isn't any deep-ocean sedimentary rocks of the Triassic.

The fossils' locations that date back to earlier in the Permian Period (Glossopteris and Mesosaurus) and also from the Triassic Period (Cynognathus and Lystrosaurus) are convincing proof that the continents to the south were at one time joined:

Chapter 4: The Climate Of The Triassic Period

The Triassic Period, especially the Early Triassic, was one of the most scorching times in the history of Earth. It was due to the fact that eruptions of volcanic activity near the close of the Permian Period had released large quantities of carbon dioxide into the air, leading to a rapid global warming. Carbon dioxide levels in the atmosphere during the Triassic were about 1750 parts for every million (ppm) that is six times higher than levels of pre-industrial times and four times more than the current level (415 ppm in 2019).

The whole Triassic Period was hot, the peak temperature was 3 million up to 4 million in the Triassic period, in the Olenekian Age, when sea temperatures in the equatorial and tropical regions exceeded the temperature of 40 degrees Celsius (104degF). Large and mobile animals were eliminated from these regions as well as a number of smaller, immobile species perished due to the Smith-Spathian extinction (discussed in chapter 10).

Conditions of arid and hot climate were prevalent throughout the Triassic:

As detailed in Chapter 3 in the Triassic Period of all Earth's landmasses joined in one supercontinent that was called Pangaea. This had profound implications for the Earth's climate.

Many regions were extremely distant from the ocean. Thus, there were a lot of large deserts. The evidence for deserts in geology can be seen in the deposits of evaporated sandstone (mineral sediments that are left behind by the evaporation of waters) as well as the red bed of sandstone.

Areas close to the ocean are likely to experience extremes in climate controlled by the ocean nearby. But, deserts and non-desert areas further away from the sea and of which there were plenty in the Triassic and Jurassic periods, have a continental climate that is characterized by extremely warm summers and cold winters. It is also believed that some regions of Pangaea could have also experienced extreme rainfall during the monsoon season.

Even though, the Triassic can be described broadly as dry and hot There were some exceptions:

* The regions close to poles were likely to have a humid and warm climate that was suitable for forest. It was also not possible to find glaciers at any pole in the Triassic.

* There appear to be a few instances of greater rainfall in the subtropical and tropical areas of the Tethys Ocean. The most well-known of these are The Carnian Pluvial Event (CPE) that occurred about 230 million years ago . It it is thought to have been initiated by global warming that ranged from 3degC (5degF) or 4degC (7degF) likely caused by volcanic activity. (This event is explained in more detail in chapter 10)

Chapter 5: Flora Of The Triassic Period

In the Carboniferous Period, the dominant trees were huge the horsetail (equisetopsid) as well as clubsmoss (lycopod) species. The species that reproduced via spores been declining in the Permian when more drought-like conditions slowly took over. The large forms of these plants were extinct by the time of the Triassic-Permian extincture, but smaller varieties survived and even thrived. For instance, neocalamites an genus of horsetails that was based on bamboo were common in humid regions that were both in of the northern as well as southern hemispheres as well as riverbanks, and along the shores of lakes.

Another common type of tree that was affected by the Triassic-Permian extinctions is Glossopteris (see chapter 11 in Before the Dinosaurs). Glossopteris was an genus of seed-ferns which were widespread throughout Gondwanaland in its Permian Period. It is important to note that numerous books suggest that Glossopteris continued to exist through its Triassic Period and perhaps even into the Jurassic Period - but this is not the case. There are fossils found in India that have been thought of as Triassic instances of Glossopteris however given that there is no evidence that Permian as well as the Triassic sedimentary rocks are mingling in the same area, this is not 100% convincing. There are other possible instances from Glossopteris of the Triassic and Jurassic might actually be similar-looking plants which have been incorrectly identified.

The demise of a variety of trees at the close of the Permian left open ecological niches for the new kinds of plant species. They were usually filled by seeds plants like ferns (pteridosperms) along with conifers. Other large plants that were successful included Cycads (plants closely resembling palms that can still be found in subtropical and tropical areas), Bennettitales (an extinct class of plant species) and Ginkgos. A lot of plants had adaptations to dry conditions (were xeromorphic) which then were the dominant species.

The typical Triassic Flora: ferns, conifers, tree-ferns and cycads horsestails, gingko tree and other horsetails:

In Laurasia forests, the areas tend to be a mix of ginkgos as well as large to medium conifers. Horsetails, bennettitales, and Cycads were more close to the surface. In northern regions, floor of the forest was likely covered in ferns. However, nearer to the equator trees and ground-growing plants were more sparse.

In Gondwanaland there was a different plant life. The seed plant Dicrodium was very widespread in certain areas, it was the sole plant to be found. Conifers, cycads and Ginkgos, and various other seed ferns like certain species from Laurasia were also prevalent in other areas. In addition, there were parts of Gondwana where huge seed ferns were growing to become the canopy on top of forests (displacing others trees) while the forest undergrowth was comprised completely of ferns, too.

Triassic flora:

There weren't any flowers-producing plants (angiosperms) in the Triassic Period, although the angiosperms' ancestral ancestors began to differ from other seed-bearing plants (gymnosperms) in the Triassic. It wasn't until later, possibly in the Jurassic Period, that the first flowering plant was discovered. The flowering plants didn't develop up until Cretaceous Period.

Chapter 6: Marine Fauna Of The Triassic Period

This chapter we'll examine a few marine species from the Triassic Period.

Plankton

In the Permian Period and for several hundred million years priorto that, the predominant phytoplankton (single-celled plants) in the oceans were Archaeplastida (red as well as green algae). After the Permian-Triassic extinctive event, there was an abrupt change and eukaryotic algae retook over as the primary phytoplankton.

Marine Invertebrates

Although corals were present from their earliest days in the Cambrian Period around 540 million years ago The oldest contemporary corals (Scleractinia) emerged in the Middle Triassic around 240 million years ago. The first scleractinians that appeared were not reef builders but were solitary or small colonies of corallite tubes that were joined at the bottom (phaceloid). The reef-building scleractinians needed another 25 million years before they could develop.

The modern coral species, Scleractinia, first appeared in the Triassic Period:

Ammonoids ("ammonites" are a particular subset of the ammonoids) are mollusks from the cephalopods which belong to the same group, which also includes cuttlefish, octopuses, squids and the nautiloids. Ammonoids are most well-known for their planar-spiral shells that were that are left by all species however there were rare ammonoids (known as heteromorphs) that had either spiraled shells, or no-spiraled shells. A single line of ammonoids survived Triassic-Permian extinction, however the survivors did diversify and ammonoids were an effective group throughout the Mesozoic.

Ammonoids:

Other marine invertebrates that belong to those of the Triassic include bivalve mollusks bryozoans, brachiopods, crinoids and the echinoderms (starfish, brittle stars sea urchins and close relatives) as well as foraminifera and gastropods. The existence of all these groups was before the Triassic however, there were significant changes. For instance brachiopods of all kinds were extinct by the end of the Permian Period and even the survivors were mostly moved by bivalve mollusks that were subject to an adaptive radiation in the Mesozoic.

Asteriacites Lumbricalis can be the trace fossils (ichnofossils) of impressions left by Triassic Brittle stars:

Fish

A variety of fish species disappeared in the Triassic-Permian extinctions, leaving only a restricted variety of families within the Triassic. Sharks with spin (acanthodians) were extinct in the Permian as well as sharks and Rays (elasmobranchs) were severely diminished in their diversity, however the ray-finned fish (actinopterygians) thrived in freshwater and saltwater environments. Teleosts were the first species of teleosts that are ray-finned fish that differ by the ability to extend their jaws to the outside of their mouth, first appeared at the time of the Early Triassic. Teleosts are today the basis of 96% of the living fish species.

Fossil Archaeosemionotus (a fish with a ray fin) in the Early Triassic:

A common species of fish seen through the Triassic and the Jurassic Period is Saurichthys. Saurichthys was a narrow, long slim fish, about one millimeter (3 feet) long. Its jaws comprised about one-third of the length. It likely attacked its prey with swift ambush attack. It is also believed to have taken a scavenge of its food, as there is evidence that suggests it was fed on the remains of marine reptiles dead.

Saurichthys:

Sauropterygian Reptiles

The sauropterygians form a class of reptiles in the water that first came into existence at the Early Triassic Epoch. While the members of the group had a variety of dimensions, body shape and appearance, they shared one thing in common the shoulders bone (pectoral girdle) that were adapted to enable efficient swimming powered with powerful strokes of the flipper.

Pachypleurosaurs

Pachypleurosaurs first came into existence in the Early Triassic about 245 million years ago. They are the oldest known sauropterygian reptiles.

Pachypleurosaurs appear to be an elongated lizard with long limbs. The head size was small, large necks, an extended body, paddle-like limbs as well as long tails. Their bodies were designed for aquatic life and weren't designed for walking on land. The earliest members of the group were around sixty centimeters (2 feet) however later members ranged in length, ranging from 20 millimeters (8 inches) to 2.7 meters (9 feet) in length.

Pachypleurosaurus edwardsi fossil:

Pachypleurosaurs had teeth that resembled pegs, that could be a sign of the diet of fish. It is also believed that at the very least, some Pachypleurosaurs were Ovoviviparous (they produced eggs that gave birth to young that hatched and formed within the uterus).

Keichousaurus fossil:

All pachypleurosaurs went extinct at the close the Triassic in the TriassicJurassic extinctions which occurred around 201 million years ago.

Nothosaurs

Nothosaurs were reptiles of the aquatic sauropterygian which lived in the Triassic Period. Their heads were small and necks that were long with an extended body, paddle-like legs (their feet are thought to be webbed) and long tails. The average size of a nothosaur was three metres (10 feet) in length, including its large neck, and long tail.

Nothosaurus mirabilis size:

Nothosaurs could have been like seals of today, catching their prey from the sea, but settling on beaches and rocks. We know for certain they had jaws armed with sharp teeth that were that were adapted to a diet consisting of fish and Squid.

Nothosaurus:

Nothosaurs can be closely associated with the pachypleurosaurs, but it is not known exactly how close they are. Some scientists consider pachypleurosaurs be part of the nothosaur group, however they consider them to be a closely related group sharing the same ancestor (a sibling taxon).

As with pachypleurosaurs too, nothosaurs also emerged relatively early in the Triassic. Similar to pachypleurosaurs nothosaurs disappeared towards the end in the Triassic in the TriassicJurassic extinctions that took place around 201 million years ago.

Placodonts

Placodonts were a species of marine reptiles who existed in the Triassic Period. They are named after their teeth (Placodontia is a reference to "tablet teeth") that in the majority of species were wide and flat. They were also tough. Their teeth are believed to have been designed for crushing shelled vertebrates, such as bivalve mollusks, brachiopods , and crustaceans. That is, virtually all placodonts are tough-shelled (they consumed a diet comprised of hard-shelled creatures).

Drawing of the jaw's upper part from Placodus gigas. Placodonts are named after the crushing teeth with flat surfaces that are clearly visible here:

Placodonts from the beginning, like Placodus were lizards that looked like stocky with long tails. They resembled today's marine iguana , but they ate brachiopods, mollusks and crustaceans, not the algae that marine iguanas consume. Placodus was approximately two meters (6.5 feet) long. Other species of this group were between 1 to three meters (3 10-foot)) in length.

Placodus:

While Placodus was protected by a few attributes, like armor that formed a by its ribs that were angled, early placodonts likely relied on their size to ward off marine predators. But in the Triassic advanced it became clear that there were larger marine predators like nothosaurs and ichthyosaurs. As a result, placodonts developed bony plates on their backs to defend their bodies. Certain species of placodonts such as Henodus and Placochelys had a carapace with bony plates that resembled the shells of sea turtles, while others like

Psephoderma were equipped with armor that resembled those of a horseshoe crab. Since placodonts ' anatomy is not with horseshoe crabs nor sea turtles these resemblances result of convergent evolution which occurs when two distinct lineages evolve in a way that they have similar structures (features with a similar shape or purpose).

Fossil of Henodus Chelyops:

While its armor is normal for a late placodont Henodus is, in many ways, the most bizarre known placodont

* This species is sole placodont to be discovered in deposits that are not marine, which is leading to notion that it might have lived in brackish or freshwater lagoons.

* Henodus has jaws that are unusual and teeth typical of an animal called a placodont. While most placodonts are designed for a life of durophagy, Henodus had only one tooth on both sides of its mouth. The other teeth replaced by beak. There are however modifications to filter feed (consuming food particles as well as other materials suspended in water through straining) such as denticles that are suited for straining and musculature that is suitable for fast jaw closing.

As with pachypleurosaurs and nothosaurus the placodonts disappeared towards the end of the Triassic in the Triassic-Jurassic extinction event, which occurred around 201 million years long ago.

Pistosaurs Plesiosaurs and Pliosaurs

In the Early Triassic, a group of carnivores with tiny heads and long necks returned to the ocean. Certain reptiles possessed knee joints that functioned and evolved into the nothosaurs and Pachypleurosaurs. However, others were completely adapted to marine life, including the pistosaurs.

The pistosaurs also differed from their nothosaur and pachypleurosaur cousins due to a more rigid backbone. Pistosaurs moved through the water with their limbs , which were now flippers instead of the use of their tails. The Pistosaurs were confined to the coastal regions, due to the pelvic bones and their shoulder (pectoral) Girdles were still weak and were not able to allow for strong strokes of swimming.

Later, possibly during later, possibly in the Late Triassic, one subgroup of pistosaurs called the plesiosaurs evolved stronger shoulder girdles and pelvis and more pointed flippers, with larger Phalanges (the bones of the digits in the hands and feet) and a shorter tail. These changes allowed plesiosaurs establish themselves in open oceans.

Traditional representation of a plesiosaur:

(scientists believe that their necks are stiff and had little flexibility, and may not have been placed this manner.)

It is generally believed to be the case that Mesozoic reptiles had cold blood as modern reptiles. This is plausible for nothosaurs however, new research has shown that pistosaurs were warm blooded (homeothermic). While there is at present, no direct evidence regarding what plesiosaurs' metabolic rate is it is likely that plesiosaurs be warm-blooded and have a high metabolic rate. In addition, they were a very successful species and it is likely that their metabolism was one of the main reasons to their great success.

Fossil plesiosaur was discovered by famed researcher Mary Anning in 1823:

in the late 19th century researchers speculated that plesiosaurs could have made their way up shores to lay eggs in a manner similar like sea turtles nowadays. It's unlikely, as it was extremely difficultsince the plesiosaurs had no functional knee or elbow joints. It is probably not feasible for the biggest species, that were as large as whales. One alternative theory is that plesiosaurs were able to give birth to live babies (were viparous) This seems to be confirmed by the fossil remains of a Polycotylus latippinus pregnant was found in 1987.

Mother and juvenile plesiosaur

Plesiosaurs are divided today into two types of body:

* Plesiosauromorphs * Plesiosauromorphs Plesiosauromorphs are animals that have large necks and long necks. They are likely to have eaten soft-bodied and hard-bodied cephalopods and fish. Their necks' length enabled them to shock groups of fish since their heads could be in contact with the fish prior to when their bodies were detected either through sight or a pressure waves. They were able to support their necks' length through the increase in bone density (cervical vertebrae).

* Pliosauromorphs - Pliosauromorphs were the most powerful predators (apex predators) in their environment and often chased or ambushed their prey. Pliosauromorphs had large heads, small necks and teeth that were capable of breaking up prey that was large.

Atychodracon is a pliosauromorph that is part of The Late Triassic and Early Jurassic:

When plesiosaurs first came to light they were initially believed that the pliosauromorphs and the plesios were closely related, but different evolutionary linesages. In conventional classifications Plesiosauria is an order that includes both types of animals, and the designations Plesiosauroidea or Pliosauroidea are applied to suborders of the various body types. Scientists now realize that a variety of long-necked groups have short-necked membersand vice versa which is why we have the current usage of the terms plesiosauromorph and the pliosauromorph. However, this shift in terms has created confusion. When people use the term "pliosaur" they are clearly referring to an animal with a shorter neck, however when they refer to "plesiosaur" they may be referring only to long-necked animals , or both short- and long-necked species.

As previously mentioned that plesiosaurs are members of the group first appeared in the Triassic Period. The first members of the group had necks that were short. Plesiosaurs were believed to have formed various forms in their Late Triassic although only a few fossils from this time have been discovered. In in the Early Jurassic, a rich range of species had emerged and scientists are trying to determine what these animals are connected to each other. The plesiosaur genus continued to exist for the remainder of the Mesozoic Era, before ending up dying towards the the Cretaceous Period.

Ichthyosaurs

Ichthyosaurs were a species of marine reptiles which first emerged during the Early Triassic around 246 million years in the past. While they are evidently originated from a terrestrial ancestor The earliest known ichthyosaurs have already been found to be diverse, and completely aquatic, and it's been difficult for scientists to pinpoint their precise origins and relationships with other reptiles. For a long time they were believed to be parareptiles with anapsids (primitive reptiles that had no skull openings other than those for nostrils and eyes) however, they are now considered as diapsids (reptiles with two additional skull openings, also known in the field of temporal fenestrae). But, their connection to other diapsids isn't clear. Up until in the 80s it was believed that sauropterygians and ichthyosaurs had similar swimming adaptations due to the common ancestor. Nowadays, the majority (but but not every) scientists believe that ichthyosaurs have evolved their swimming skills independently of sauropterygians.

The first-known ichthyosaur related to Cartorhynchus who lived approximately two million years before. Cartorhynchus isn't itself an ichthyosaur and isn't an ichthyosaur ancestral ancestor, however it is believed as being closely related with the first ichthyosaur. Cartorhynchus was forty centimeters (16 inches) in length and weighed around 2 kilograms (4.4 lbs). It was likely amphibious, and could move on land in the same way seals nowadays. Its adaptations to life underwater include the flippers of its limbs as well as shortened hindlimbs. the weight of its bones, which would have affected the animal's buoyancy, allowing it the ability to swim into the water.

Cartorhynchus was first discovered in 2014, however since 1959, another category of animals closely related to ichthyosaurs is also recognized for a while: the Hupehsuchia. Hupehsuchia are described in greater detail in the following sections, but knowing of their existence hasn't allowed us to understand the origins of ichthyosaurs, as we don't know what hupehsuchians evolved .

The earliest ichthyosaurs were thought to resembled lizards with fins. They had bodies that were elongated and most likely, swam with their entire body as if they were the invertebral eel (anguilliform movement). Also, they had a bizarre mix of primitive and advanced traits. On the one hand, their legs had been transformed into flippers, and they likely were warm-blooded (homeothermic) and likely gave birth to live babies (viviparous). On the other hand their shoulder and pelvis (pectoral) and girdles and their vertebrae were identical to the girdles of terrestrial animals and were over-engineered to accommodate marine life.

Ichthyosaurs with more advanced technology began to appear around 245 million years ago. This included:

* Mixosaurs - The mixosaurs inwardly looked like fish. They had an elongated head with a shorter trunk with a longer tail as well as flippers that had phalanges of many and a dorsal fin.

* Merriamosaurs - Merriamosaurs are akin to dolphins. They can be distinguished by the narrower front-flippers, and the smaller fingers on their flippers.

* Cymbospondylus - Cymbospondylus was a huge animal that could grow upwards of 10

metres (33 feet) in length. It resembled a sea snake since it didn't have an dorsal fin as well as a the fluffed tail. It likely swam by wriggling its body one side of the other. The limbs could be used to stabilize and, if required to slow down. Cymbospondylus does not fit into any easy classifications and doesn't fit into any of the categories of ichthyosaurs. As such, researchers believe it could be a different species from the other ichthyosaurs at a relatively early stage in its evolutionary journey.

Mixosaurus:

Cymbospondylus skeleton:

At the Carnian as well as Norian Ages of the Triassic Some ichthyosaurs had enormous size. Shonisaurus species reached sizes of up to 15 metres (49 feet). A different kind of ichthyosaur, Shastasaurus, may have been 21 meters (69 feet) in length. Both Shonisaurus as well as Shastasaurus were relatively slim bodies for ichthyosaurs, and likely lacked dorsal fins.

Shastasaurus sikanniensis:

At the time of during the Late Triassic, ichthyosaurs had achieved their greatest variety and were able to fill a range of niches in the ecology. These niches comprised both predators at the apex as well as predators which were able to eat smaller prey. Ichthyosaurs utilized a range of feeding methods, including eating rams (also called lung feeding) which occurs where the predator takes on the prey as well as the water around it suction feeding, which is when predators suck prey into their mouths, and durophagous food, which is when prey is eaten with hard shells.

Ichthyosaur fossil. The epidermis was preserved , forming an outline of the body of the animal:

The largest ichthyosaurs went extinct prior to the Rhaetian Age which was the last period that was the Triassic. The reasons for this are not known however, it is possible that it been due to the increased competition from plesiosaurs sharks, and Teleosts. However, a variety of species of ichthyosaurs lived through the Triassic. The Triassic-Jurassic extinctions event further decreased the number of ichthyosaur species. However, following it, they began to re-diversify with some species continuing throughout the entire Jurassic Period and into the Cretaceous Period. The last ichthyosaur likely went extinct towards the close in the Cenomanian Age in the Late Cretaceous during the Cenomanian-Turonian extinction (see my work, Dinosaurs & Other Animals of the Cretaceous).

Hupehsuchia

Hupehsuchians are a family of reptiles living in the water that were in existence for a brief period (a couple of million years, at the most) during the Triassic Early Epoch. Fossils were discovered approximately 248 million to 247.2 million years earlier. They were discovered as early as 1959 within China. The group's name comes from the Hubei province located in central China.

Hupehsuchians are very similar to ichthyosaurs. However, this wasn't discovered for a long time before the possibility was never consideredbecause hupehsuchians employed an entirely different method to propel themselves in the water.

Hupehsuchus nanchangensis:

Hupehsuchians were spindle-shaped with a body, limbs used to paddle the water, and an extended jaws and skull which were devoid of teeth (are dentally edentulous). The most common features are shared between ichthyosaurs and Hupehsuchians were their pointed snouts as well as multidactyly (having at least five fingers and toes). Hupehsuchians were likely to have been aquatic creatures, as their bodies weren't suited for being on the land. Researchers believe that hupehsuchians are living (giving the birth of live children) because other methods to reproduction could have been challenging, and we are aware that ichthyosaurs were viviparous.

Thalattosaurs

Thalattosaurs were a family of marine reptiles which lived throughout the Middle and late Triassic Epochs. They were akin to long slender lizards that had large, flattened tails. However, their relation to other groups is not clear. The biggest thalattosaurs were over four metres (13 feet) in length.

A subgroup of thalattosaurs called Askeptosauroidea has large, narrow skulls that have nostrils close to the sockets of their eyes. A second subgroup called Thalattosauroidea has distinctive snouts that are downturned. The two subgroups share similarities, for instance, in the skull's design that clearly indicate their close ties.

Thalattosaurs disappeared at the close in the Triassic in the TriassicJurassic extinctions that took place around 201 millions of years ago.

Chapter 7: Terrestrial And Freshwater Fauna Of The Triassic Period

This chapter we'll look at some of the freshwater and terrestrial fauna from the Triassic Period. Dinosaurs, as well as their closest relatives are dealt with separately in Chapter 8.

Insects

There is a solitary evidence of fossils from insects dating to in the Early Triassic, although some fossils have been discovered in the eastern region of Europe. In addition, we have some fossils, specifically of beetles from The Kuznetsk Basin and the Korotaikha Basin Both of them are situated in Russia.

Concerning Triassic beetles:

* We are aware that three of the four suborders currently in existence of beetles existed during the Triassic: Archostemata, Adephaga and Polyphaga. Notably, the earliest fossil discovered of the living fourth infraorder Myxophaga was discovered in The Early Cretaceous.

* The late Triassic beetles are believed to include species that were aldophagous (algae devouring) species and mycetophagous (fungus

eating) species, as well as the water beetles that hunted predators.

The first known instances of two major insect groups first appeared within the Triassic: Diptera (flies) and Hymenoptera (the group which includes bees, ants as well as wasps). The existence of flies at the present time is now known due to the discovery of an individual fossil wing that measures 10 millimeters (0.4 millimeters) across that was discovered in Australia.

Spiders

We know that our closest relatives of spiders, called the Uraraneida were around 3 million years ago, during the Devonian Period. But they did not have the Uraraneida didn't have spinnerets (the silk-producing organ that is found inside spiders) and was unable to produce silk. The oldest spiders to produce silk were Mesothelae. The Mesothelae first was discovered about 300 million years back in the Late Carboniferous Period and a few of their members are still alive until today. The difference is that Mesothelae distinguish themselves from modern-day spiders by having their spinnerets are situated under the abdomen's middle instead of at the top.

Spiders with spinnerets located at the back of the abdomen. Mygalomorphae (also called Orthognatha) as well as Araneomorphae (also also known as Labidognatha) first appeared during the Early Triassic about 250 million years ago. It is worth noting that, as mentioned in Before the Dinosaurs, some older sources incorrectly classify the Carboniferous species Megarachne as a mygalomorph that was an early spider, but it's actually an Eurypterid (sea scorpion).

Lungfish

There are currently only six species of lungfish. they only exist within Africa, Australia and South America. The first lungfish evolved time ago in the Early Devonian about 416 million years ago. The species that survives are the only remaining remains of an extremely diverse group.

Lungfish was particularly productive during their time in the Triassic Period when they populated numerous lakes, rivers and freshwater bodies. We are aware of this since fossils of the lungfish's dental plates are frequently located within Triassic rocks.

Ceratodus first is recorded in fossils in it's Late Triassic about 227 million years ago.

Like African as well as South American lungfish do today in the present, some Triassic lungfish species like Ceratodus and Arganodus lived in a state of dormancy (estivated as well as be spelled as aestivated, aestivated, or) within underground burrows in the dry season, awaiting rain to were on the way in the monsoon.

Amphibians

The earliest species of tetrapods (four-legged vertebrates) were evolved from the sarcopterygian (ray-finned) fish in the Devonian Period, and they went on to evolve throughout the Carboniferous as well as Permian Periods. There were a variety of amphibians died out in the Permian-Triassic extinction, however some survived, such as reptiliomorphs as well as the temnospondyl and reptiliomorph groups.

The reptiliomorphs are the species that share the most recent common ancestral lineage with amniotes (animals who lay eggs on the ground or keep their eggs in the mother) as opposed to living amphibians. While they are not amniotes reptiliomorphs could be classified as amphibian reptiles. Reptiliomorphs who survived into Triassic include Chroniosuchia. These were predators that hunted on rivers, resembling crocod and often with armor on their backs.

Chroniosuchia was not able to survive for very long during the Triassic and then went extinct in only a couple of million years.

Temnospondyls were a diverse species of amphibians that arose within the Carboniferous (see Before the Dinosaurs). At the time of their time in the Triassic Period, they had generally disappeared from the terrestrial ecosystems with reptiles. Yet, temnospondyls remained common in semi-aquatic and aquatic habitats.

Parotosuchus is a temnospondyl in the Early Triassic:

One temnospondyl group, the trematosaurs, had great success during the Early Triassic. They were medium-sized and had skulls with narrow sides and in some instances long snouts which evolved to eat fish. Most trematosaurs were in freshwater habitats, however one particular family, the Trematosauridae moved to the oceans and evolved into marine animals - a life style which is rare for amphibians.

Aphaneramma was a temnospondyl that was about 2 metres (7 feet) long, that was found within the Triassic:

Another temnospondyl group which had some success during The Early Triassic were the capitosaurs. These creatures resided in freshwater lakes and rivers, and they ate fish, playing an ecological role similar to the one that crocodiles play nowadays. Certain capitosaurs expanded to massive sizes. The largest was Mastodonsaurus giganteus that grew to six meters (20 feet) in length. It was the longest amphibian that has been identified to scientists. As crocodiles developed during the Middle Triassic, Capitosaurs went into declineand disappeared at the conclusion in the Triassic.

Mastodonsaurus:

Other groups of temnospondyl amphibians have been most successful during the Late Triassic. They include the metoposaurs, as well as plagiosaurs.

Metoposaurs are typically 1.5 millimeters (5 feet) in length. They are distinguished from the other similar mastodonsaurs based on the fact that they have eyes that are positioned farther forward on the snout. The most well-known of the metoposaurs is Metoposaurus that was three metres (10 feet) in length and weighed up to 450 pounds (1,000 lbs). Metoposaurus fossils are frequently located within "mass graves" which have been seen as proof of the creatures forming a group because their pools drained out during prolonged droughts. A different hypothesis may be"mass graves" are not evidence of a collective effort "mass grave" is just a collection of bodies that were washed together by the currents of rivers.

* Plagiosaurs had an unflattened skull and body. They had thin and weak legs but a huge head , with jaws covered with teeth resembling needles. Their heads were small and wide , and roughly semicircular in form. Plagiosaurs are believed to be almost completely aquatic and had internal gills. They were believed to have swam in the bottoms of rivers and lakes and were fed by snatching prey like fish and other species. In addition to their gills that are flat and flat and gills, their adaptations to the living in the bottom of the water include a unique jaw joint (the atlanto-occipital joint) which makes it easier for animals to open their mouths by lifting their cranium instead of dropping its jaw in the typical manner of species.

Gerrothorax Pulcherrimus was a palagiosaur from the Middle and Late Triassic. It measured about 1 one meter (3.3 feet) long and believed to have utilized its large eyes that were facing upwards to look for prey when it lay at the bottom of riverbeds and lakes.

The general consensus is that temnospondyls had a high success as semi-aquatic predators in the Triassic and were able to dominate numerous ecological niches. There were numerous species, and temnospondyls were common in Antarctica that was surrounded by temperate forests in the early days.

Plagiosaurus:

The end in the Triassic Period, things changed. The majority of temnospondyl species perished in the Triassic-Jurassic extinction. But a handful of trematosaurs , as well as a few members of a different group called the brachyopoids survived the extinction event , and through the Jurassic Period. The trematosaurus ended its life after the Jurassic but a small number of brachyopoids remained alive through the Cretaceous Period.

Another group of amphibians to mention is Lissamphibia which encompasses the modern amphibians. Lisssamphibians first appeared in early in Early Triassic, one such species being Triadobatrachus massinoti that was alive for about 250 million years prior. Triadobatrachus massinoti was around 10 centimeters (4 inches) long , and was outwardly similar to the inwardly a frog. However, there were significant differences . Triadobatrachus was a vertebral tiger with more vertebrae than modern-day frogs, had a shorter tail and could not leap like modern frogs.

Triadobatrachus massinoti:

Parareptiles

Parareptiles, also known as primitive reptiles that have skulls that have no openings apart from those for the eyes and nostrils (they don't have the temporal fenestrae). This is referred to as an Anapsid skull.

The Procolophonidae are a group of parareptiles which first appeared during the Late Permian. They were able to survive the Triassic-Permian extinction up to the end that of the Triassic Period. The Procolophonidae were lizard-like, but weren't related to them. They had broad, low legs, short tails, and some were fitted with spikes over their heads to guard against predators. At the start of Triassic the majority of types belonging to Procolophonidae were sharp-toothed. They also ate insects (were insectivores) however, later species had teeth that were broader suggesting a shift to an herbivore diet.

Turtles

When we study the skulls of Turtles and discover that they have Anapsid skulls that resemble those of parareptiles. That are skulls that have no openings other than the ones for the nose and eyes. One of the major paleontological questions is whether turtles evolved from parareptiles or if they originated through diapsid reptiles (reptiles with two openings inside the skull referred to as temporal fenestrae) and then were unable to find (reversion) the temporal fenestrae.

The first known animal believed to be a relative of turtles was Eunotosaurus which was found in the Permian (see Before the Dinosaurs). While Eunotosaurus is a tad different from other dinosaurs, its characteristics appear to be similar to the modern turtles, it's not clear if it's an animal that is a diapsid or parareptile (since only a small amount of skull remains have been discovered) and even if it is related to turtles in any way.

The first undisputed turtle relatives come from the Triassic and are diapsids. Early turtle relatives did not have aquatic adaptations and are likely to have been semi-aquatic or terrestrial creatures.

* Pappochelys Rosanae is an diapsid reptile, which was around 250 million years ago in the Middle Triassic and appears to be closely related to the turtle ancestors. The skeleton of the animal bears distinct features that resemble turtles, however there are some significant distinctions, such as being able to see temporal

and fenestrae, as well as of teeth within the jaws of the animal (present-day turtles do not have teeth). Pappochelys are also intermediate in shape in between Odontochelys (see the next section below) and Eunotosaurus and Eunotosaurus, suggesting that Eunotosaurus is a turtle's an ancestor in the end.

* Odontochelys semitestacea is a stem-turtle. This implies that it is closer to turtles than any other living animal group. This species lived for about two hundred million years back in the Late Triassic. While it was clearly a turtle however, it was only equipped with the bottom part of a turtle's shell (the plastron) and likely lacked the an upper layer of armor (the carapace). Furthermore, Odontochelys semitestacea had teeth in both its lower and upper jaws and had distinct skeletal differences from modern-day turtles.

* Proganochelys quenstedti is also a stem-turtle. It is the first stem-turtle to have a fully-formed shell that lived for about 200 million years ago during the Triassic Late Epoch. It was approximately 1 meters (3 feet) long and featured many characteristics that are similar to modern turtles that included an armored shell that had both carapace and plastron, and a mouth that resembled a beak rather than teeth.

Proganochelys had a tail that was long that was different from modern turtles. The tail was fitted with spikes throughout its length , and a club at the bottom.

Proganochelys:

Lepidosauromorpha

Lepidosauromorpha is the name given to the group of diapsid reptiles closer to lizards, but not to archosaurs (archosaurs are discussed in the following section). The Lepidosauromorpha group likely evolved from other reptiles during the Permian Period or Triassic Period However, scientists aren't completely certain of the exact time of the divergence.

The tuatara is the sole remaining species of Rhynchocephalia:

Lepidosauromorpha can contain up to four reptile subgroups:

* Pantestudines * Pantestudines Pantestudines are the class of reptiles which includes tortoises and turtles as well in their extinct ancestors as well as closely related species (possibly including sauropterygians, see chapter 6). This group's inclusion within Lepidosauromorpha is not without controversy, since there are a variety of scientists who disagree on whether

they belong in this category or even if they are diapsids.

* Kuehneosauridae * Kuehneosauridae Kuehneosauridae are a group of diapsid reptiles which extinct and were present in the Triassic Period. Kuehneosauridae were lizard-like insectivores. Some members of this group were able to have ribs that protruded away from the body and were connected by a membrane of skin. The membrane could have functioned as a wing, allowing individuals of this family jump from trees and other to glide. Like Pantestudines Some scientists believe that Kuehneosauridae shouldn't be considered part of Lepidosauromorpha.

* Rhynchocephalia * Rhynchocephalia Rhynchocephalia are a different kind of reptiles that resemble lizards. They are distinguished by a number of features that differentiate them from lizards. These consist of the third "eye" at the top of their heads as well as distinct features in their skull (especially the skull) as well as the teeth. Rhynchocephalia used to be a successful species of animal that had a large share of ecological niches currently being occupied by lizards. The group even had aquatic members in their Jurassic as well as the Cretaceous periods. One kind (with 2

subspecies) of Rhynchocephalia is still alive to this day that is the Tuatara (scientific terms: Sphenodon punctatus punctatus as well as Sphenodon punctatus guntheri).

* Squamata * Squamata Squamata is the name given to the group of reptiles, which includes snakes, lizards amphisbaenians (worm lizards) and Mosasaurs (extinct marine reptiles from earlier in the Cretaceous Period - see Dinosaurs & Other Animals of the Cretaceous). The first fossils that have been discovered of skinks, geckos, and snakes are found within the Middle Jurassic, and other groups, like iguanians or varanoids (monitor lizards) are found in the Cretaceous however, as we know that Rhynchocephalia has been separated from Squamata during the Triassic and we are certain that Squamata is also dated from the Triassic. The fossil evidence for Squamata during the Triassic isn't extensive. There is a fossilized jaw from India known as Tikiguania estsi, which could be Triassic in its origin (or could not be) There is also an fossil from Italy known as Megachirella which dates back to the age of 240 million years, that recent research suggests is an one of the early members of Squamata.

Groups' relations in Lepidosauromorpha:

Therapsids

As we will see in chapter 11, Before the Dinosaurs, synapsids (amniotes with just a only a single pair of temporal-fenestrae) as well as their successors called therapsids were the largest terrestrial megafauna (large creatures) from the Permian Period.

Synapsid principal groups beginning as early as through the Middle Permian onwards:

Most of the species of therapsid went out in the Triassic-Permian extinction event. However, three distinct groups of therapsids remained throughout the Triassic Period.

* Dicynodonts

* Therocephalians

* Cynodonts

Though they lasted for a time, the dicynodonts and therocephalians died out, leaving the only living descendants. However the cynodonts have not only lived for a short time however, some of them later developed into mammals. We'll now look at every one of them individually.

Dicynodonts

Dicynodonts were a very productive and varied group. Though all were herbivores, individuals of this group differed significantly in dimensions. The smallest was around an inch in size, which is about the same as a rat , while the largest was nearly as large than an elephant.

Dicynodonts were short-bodied with barrel-shaped bodies, small tails, and strong legs. They typically held their rear limbs straight and their front legs were bent at their elbow. Their skulls were small but sturdy and had large temporal fenestrae, to which were attached jaw muscles that were strong and powerful. The majority of dicynodonts had no teeth, except for the tusks. It is also believed the fact that their hair was present, and they were thought to be the homeothermic (warm-blooded).

Dicynodonts first emerged at their earliest stages in the Middle Permian but only four lineages survived the Triassic-Permian extinctions: Lystrosaurus, Kombuisaia, Myosaurus and a group dubbed the Kannemeyeriiformes.

Lystrosaurus:

Lystrosaurus was extremely effective for a short period in its time in the Early Triassic Epoch - in certain fossil sediments, Lystrosaurus accounts for 95 percent of all terrestrial vertebrates that were found. Yet, Lystrosaurus, as well as Kombuisaia and Myosaurus all perished within a couple of million years.

Lystrosaurus fossil:

On the other hand the Kannemeyeriiformes flourished and changed throughout the Triassic. They were the most dominant large herbivores from the Early Triassic (Olenekian Age) until the close of the Middle Triassic.

Skull of Kannemeyeria A large dicynodont from Kannemeyeria, a large dicynodont belonging to the Kannemeyeriiformes family:

Kannemeyeriiformes were typically in the range of porcine and an ox. One kind, Lisowicia bojani, weighed 9 tonnes and was the same size as an elephant. Lisowicia bojani is also unique as it is the only known dicynodont species that holds all four limbs in an upright position underneath the body instead of the standard semi-erect posture that is common to the majority of dizynodonts.

Kannemeyeriiformes began to decline during early Late Triassic. Through the beginning in the Late Triassic, they had been mostly displaced by the group of herbivore cynodonts known as the Traversodontidae and by reptiles called archosauromorphs or Rhynchosaurs (see further below). There is a general belief that the Kannemeyeriiformes, as well as the entire dicynodont genus were extinct by the end in the Triassic Period. However skull fragments discovered within Queensland, Australia are claimed by some scientists to be proof of a dicynodont living up to that of the Cretaceous Period.

Placerias was an ancestor of the Kannemeyeriiformes family was among the last dicynodonts in late Triassic. Late Triassic:

Therocephalians

Therocephalians were a separate type of therapsids that emerged in the Permian Period. The majority of therocephalians were extinct in the Triassic-Permian extinction event however a tiny subset that scientists refer to as Eutherocephalia was able to survive through the Triassic. The remaining was extinct by Middle Triassic, probably because changes in climate and the competition from other groups.

Therocephalians have a variety of traits with Cynodonts (and the mammalian ancestors of cynodonts). This includes the temporal opening that is connected to jaw muscles larger, a smaller number of the phalanges (finger as well as toe bone) as well as a secondary palate (allowing breathing and chewing simultaneously) and evidence of the presence of warm blood. In reality it is so similar to the evolution paths of therocephalians and cynodonts , that at times, scientists believed that both were the ancestors of various species of primitive mammals. Researchers now realize this isn't true and that mammals evolved only from the cynodonts. The shared traits and the evolutionary pathways of therocephalians as well as cynodonts are now attributed partly to common ancestors, and also to convergence in evolution.

Bauria was one of the carnivores, or insectivore, which lived during the Early Triassic:

Cynodonts

Cynodonts were the final Therapsids group to be discovered. The first fossils of cynodonts can be discovered within Late Permian rocks. Cynodonts are likely to be at homeothermic (warm-blooded) as they had many advanced mammal-like characteristics. They had the mandible reduced to one bone, which allowed different jawbones to be moved into the ear to facilitate better hearing as well as the repositioning of nostrils from the front of the mouth, and the formation of a secondary palate (allowing breathing and chewing simultaneously).

Cynodonts that are the most sophisticated have been classified as Eucynodonts. This group comprises a range of nonmammalian subgroups like the cynognathids (all comprised of carnivores) and traversodonts (all of which are herbivores) and two smaller and very mammal-like subgroups tritheledontids (also called ictidosaurs) and tritylodontids.

Cynognathus skeleton:

(Cynognathus was one of the cynognathid Cynodont from the Middle Triassic)

The eucynodonts are believed to have given birth to mammals. It's a bit arbitrary as to what species are classified as mammals and those that are classified as nonmammals with mammal-like traits. A common definition employed is crown-group mammals which encompasses the most modern ancestral ancestor of all living mammals and all of that descendants of that ancestral ancestor.

Being born in the Permian Period, cynodonts survived both the Triassic-Permian extinction event as well as the Triassic-Jurassic extinction. Cynodonts that were not mammals lived for around 80 million years, and ended up extincting in this period of the Middle Jurassic. Mammaliamorphs that resembled mammal mammaliamorphs first emerged in early Late

Triassic and the earliest members of the crown-group mammals were first discovered in the Jurassic's Early Epoch.

Oligokyphus was a tiny Cynodont from The Late Triassic and Early Jurassic. It was approximately fifty centimeters (20 inches) long. The mammaliamorph is classified since although it had similar features to mammals, it didn't include all the typical jaw and skull features of mammals:

In the Triassic Therapsids (including their mammaliamorph ancestors) were gradually displace as the predominant group of land animals that were large. Therapsids and mammaliamorphs who survived were smaller, nocturnal and, in some cases, insectivores. These events are referred to in the Triassic takeover. This bottleneck, also known as nocturnal has profound effects on the evolution of mammalian species which included mammalian anatomy and behavior, as well as physiology - for example, today, the majority of mammal species are tiny nocturnal creatures. The animals which displaced the therapsids and mammaliamorphs is known as archosaurs and archosauromorphs.

Archosaurs as well as Archosauromorpha

Archosaurs constitute the crown group, which includes one of the most modern common ancestors living birds, as well as living crocodilians, as well as the descendants of that ancestor. This the crocodiles as well as its extinct relatives (Pseudosuchia) as well as the birds as well as their relatives extinct (Avemetatarsalia) including non-avian dinosaurs as well as pterosaurs.

Archosaurs are characterized by a number of traits (synapomorphies) which are passed down from an ancestor who was common to all. They have open skulls that are in forward of eyes (antorbital Fenestrae) and open jaws (mandibular Fenestrae) teeth that are placed in sockets (although certain species eventually became toothless) and the knob (fourth trochanter) in the thighbone (femur) to which muscles are connected.

Archosauromorpha is a slightly larger group of animals which includes all archosaurs as with their cousins which are closer to archosaurs , but less so to lepidosaurs (lizards or snakes, tuataras and so on.). Archosauromorpha certainly includes a variety of archosaur-like species, including Rhynchosaurs (a group of herbivores with stocky necks who lived in the Triassic Period), tanystropheids (a family that is known for its extremely long necks) and allokotosaurs (another herbivore species) however there are some groups which's inclusion in Archosauromorpha is more uncertain. A few of the groups that are included by some scientists in Archosauromopha however, others feel shouldn't be included include:

* Pantestudines * Pantestudines Pantestudines are the category of reptiles which includes tortoises and turtles as well in their extinct ancestors as well as their close cousins (possibly which includes Sauropterygians). As mentioned in this section about Lepidosauromorpha some scientists have included Pantestudines in this group. Some scientists believe that tortoises and turtles ought to be included in the parareptiles. The general consensus is that anatomical evidence suggests Pantestudines are included within Lepidosauromorpha , but genetic evidence suggests Pantestudines ought to be added in Archosauromorpha.

* Kuehneosauridae * Kuehneosauridae Kuehneosauridae are a species of diapsid reptiles extinct that were present in the Triassic Period, and which were parachuted or glided around onto "wings" constructed from skin membranes that were attached to long ribs.

Some scientists believe Kuehneosauridae are appropriate to include in Archosauromorpha however others believe Kuehneosauridae are best placed in Lepidosauromorpha.

* Thalattosaurs - Thalattosaurs are a species comprising aquatic reptiles (see chapter 6) which lived in their time in the Middle as well as the Late Triassic. The origin of thalattosaurs is not clear, but certain scientists have them included in Archosauromorpha.

* Choristodera * Choristodera Choristodera are a species that includes semi-aquatic reptiles. Fossils belonging to this group have been discovered from in the Jurassic Period through to the Miocene Epoch of the Neogene Period but it is thought that the group may have was formed earlier, during the Permian Period. There is only one Triassic fossil found in southwest England Pachystropheus that could belong to the group. Choristodera share features with archosauromorphs as well as Lepidosauromorpha which makes it unclear what they evolved from.

* Drepanosaurs The drepanosaurs comprise an unusual group of reptiles which lived in the late Triassic Epoch. They were limbs that grasped (similar to the cameleon's) as well as an elongated tail (often end with claws) and

triangular skulls that often ended with toothless beaks. There has been a lot of debate regarding how drepanosaurs could be connected to other groups of diapsids.

Champsosaurus was a species of the Choristodera family that lived in the Late Cretaceous and Paleogene Periods:

In the Triassic archosaurs, as well as archosauromorphs gradually took over as the predominant group of land animals large and massive and displaced therapsids (and their mammaliamorph relatives) from the ecological niches they occupied. These events are referred to as Triassic takeover. Triassic takeover.

It's not completely evident why archosaurs as well as archosauromorphs have achieved this level of success, although a number of explanations have been offered. These theories include:

Archosauromorphs and archosaurs have made greater progress towards straight positions than therapsids. This could have provided them with greater endurance compared to sprawling reptiles that move their bodies in a sideways direction when walking. Reptiles that are sprawled struggle to move and breathe simultaneously (this is known as Carrier's constrict). The problem with this theory is that it does not consider the Triassic change was initiated when animals from both the archosaur and therapsid lines were limbs that were semi-erect or sprawling.

* Archosauromorphs, archosaurs and archos better respiration mechanisms than therapsids. In the Permian there was a decrease in oxygen levels in the atmosphere, so better respiration could have been a significant benefit.

* The conditions of the Triassic were mostly dry and archosauromorphs as well as archosaurs could have been better in conserving water than other therapsids. In particular, diapsids typically release waste as the uric acid paste, which contains only a only a small amount of water. However, therapsids and mammals expel waste as dilute urine, which contains lots of water. Furthermore mammals, and possibly therapsids as well, also had numerous glands on their skin that lead to water loss however diapsids do not have glands (aglandular) the skin.

Comparison of spreading (left) and pilon-erect (center) and the erect (right) poses:

Sprawling postures are common in all early amniotes. Pillar-erect postures are seen in some archosaur species like aetosaurs and rauisuchoids. These postures can be seen in other archosaur families like dinosaurs as well as in mammals.

In this article, we will discuss a few of the archosaurs as well as archosauromorphs that were discovered in the Triassic Period.

Protorosaurs

Protorosaurs comprise a variety of archosauromorph reptiles found during the Late Permian and Early Triassic. The most distinctive features of their species were spines that extended backwards as well as necks with long necks, which were supported by vertebrae with lengthened. Protorosaurs also had gaps in the bones close to the jaw joint. This caused their skulls to resemble those of Lizards.

Since protorosaurs are so varied, certain scientists believe that the group is traditionally classified in a polyphyletic fashion (including species which aren't closely related since they don't share an immediate common ancestral ancestor) or in a paraphyletic manner (omitting certain species that are descendents of the same common ancestral lineage). In the end, there has been a lot of discussion regarding the groups that are added to Protorosauria and also about how to define the term in a more precise manner.

Protorosaurus:

The protorosaur with the earliest known record is Protorosaurus that lived in the Permian-Late Permian Epoch. Protorosaurus was two meters (6.6 feet) tall, with an extended neck, a slim body as well as long legs. Protorosaurus was extinct towards the end of the Permian however, its closest cousin Czatkowiella was alive in Czatkowiella's Early Triassic Epoch.

Protorosaurus skeleton:

Two protorosaurs appear to have developed independently glider-like adaptations in the Triassic:

* Mecistotrachelos was a species that lived within the Late Triassic, glided on an elongated membrane that was supported by rib bones. Based on the small tooth conical, Mecistotrachelos may be an insectivore. It's also believed to have been an arboreal (lived among trees) because its hindlimbs and toes are well-suited for grasping branches and trees.

* Sharovipteryx was also a glider reptile in during the Late Triassic. It was only discovered from one fossil and glided on a triangular wing ("delta wings") around its hindlimbs and pelvis. A close cousin of Sharovipteryx known as Ozimek volans, also believed to be an glider has

been discovered. An in-depth study of Ozimek volans has revealed that it has a close relationship to protorosaurs with long necks (described below) which means that Sharovipteryx could be related to it as well.

Tanystropheids were a group comprised of marine reptiles that existed throughout the Triassic Period, only becoming extinct towards the close of the Triassic in the Triassic-Jurassic extinct event. They are believed to have been a broad group , and their fossils can be found in areas that were previously part of the coast in the Tethys Ocean. But, certain fossils can also be found in terrestrial deposits within the present western part of North America. This means that there were not all species that were aquatic or semi-aquatic.

The most noticeable characteristic of the tanystropheids is their long necks. Sometimes, their necks could be many meters long, which was more than the other parts of the animal's body. The necks of these animals were stiff and were supported by long vertebrae.

Tanystropheus is possibly the most well known tanystropheid. It was found in the Middle Triassic Epoch and was around six metres (20 feet) long. The neck of the animal was 3 millimeters (9.8 feet) long, and it was caped with a small head. It is believed that it consumed a piscivorous diet (fish taking). The evidence for Tanystropheus as a piscivore consists of the evidence that the animal was interlocked with conical teeth, which appear to have been designed to grasp slippery prey and that fish scales as well as cephalopod remains have been found near the stomach areas within Tanystropheus fossils.

Though many tanystropheids have developed longer necks through the extension of their vertebrae are believed to have developed long necks using an alternative method, namely the addition of additional vertebrae. Dinocephalosaurus is one such animal the marine tanystropheid which was alive in the middle of the Middle Triassic Epoch around about 245 million years ago . It was also 244 million years ago.

Dinocephalosaurus was 3 to 3.5 metres (9.8 up to 11.5") in length and the neck around 1.7 metres (5.6 feet) long. It was a paddle-like creature and is believed as having given birth to young.

Estimated size of Dinocephalosaurus:

Other animals that may be protorosaurs include the elusive and bizarre drepanosaurs that resemble chameleons, Pterosaurs, fly-flying reptiles (described below) as well as Longisquama a reptile that is not well understood that is part of The Middle as well as Late Triassic.

Longisquama reconstructions based on impression and bones was found to be:

Longisquama is only known from a skeleton that is badly preserved and a handful of fossil impressions. Its name is derived from "long Scales" and it is identified by what appears to be oddly extended scales in its rear. These "scales" have been perceived in various scientific studies as feather-like, but they are not feather-like but rather ribbon-like scales, or perhaps just plants fronds in the mix with the skull.

Pterosaurs

Pterosaurs are winged reptiles that first emerged during the Late Triassic Epoch about 228 million years ago. They were actually the first vertebrate species to have powered flight even though there had glided vertebrates like Coelurosauravus from The Permian Period (see Before the Dinosaurs) and Kuehneosauridae (see the previous paragraph) which first been discovered during early Early Triassic.

The wings of a pterosaur were made up of skin membrane and muscles that stretched from the animal's ankle up to a hugely extended fourth finger. The earliest species, such as the Triassic species were equipped with jaws which were fully toothed as well as longer tails, however, later species may have shorter tails that were toothless. Certain species of pterosaurs had a membrane that was stretched between their legs that was possibly linked to their tail (the member is referred to as the uropatagium, or cruropatagium, depending on whether it was connected with the tail).

A comparison of the wings structures of an Pterosaur (left) and bat (center) and bird (right):

There are many common misconceptions about pterosaurs.

Pterosaurs can be described by the general populace in the form of "flying dinosaurs". However, this isn't the case. While it is true pterosaurs were around the same timeframe as extinct dinosaurs but they weren't dinosaurs.

Pterosaurs are often incorrectly called "pterodactyls". Pterodactyl is used correctly to refer to the specific type of pterosaur Pterodactylus antiquus (which was the first pterosaur species ever to be scientifically named and described) or to individuals belonging to the Pterodactyloidea group of Pterosaurs (see Dinosaurs & Other Animals of the Jurassic).

* Pterosaurs have been considered to be only eating fish (piscivorous) and playing the same function in Mesozoic ecology to what seabirds play in the present. Although it is true there were a few pterosaurs that were piscivores, it's thought that the vast majority were carnivores, omnivores or insectivores. There are also theories that they may be moluskivores (specialized for eating bivalve-shaped mollusks and gastropods, brachiopods, and cephalopods) as well as suspension feeders as well as some animals that could not fly and were mostly concentrated on terrestrial carnivores.

* In films where pterosaurs appear, they are usually depicted as lifting their prey using their feet in a similar manner like how contemporary birds of prey utilize their feet. Pterosaurs didn't have feet that were prehensile and were not equipped to grip with their feet in this manner.

Pterodactylus antiquus Pterosaur, a pterosaur of Jurassic Period:

Scientists aren't quite sure of about the source of Pterosaurs' origins. Different theories have been proposed which include that they may originate from protorosaurs, or from close relatives of the early archosaurs.

Scientists do not have a full understanding of the mechanisms that allowed pterosaurs to fly. Certain scientists have suggested they could only fly because of the oxygen-rich atmosphere of Mesozoic However, other scientists disagree. It's also difficult to comprehend how they flew away and in the event that the cold blooded (ectothermic) and cold-blooded, it is unlikely that larger pterosaurs could be able to become flying. Numerous scientists are now convinced that pterosaurs were warm blooded (homeothermic).

Pterosaurs were present for the majority time in the Mesozoic. They first emerged at the end of the Late Triassic about 228 million years ago. Members of the group lived across all of the Jurassic as well as the Cretaceous Periods before finally becoming extinct 66 million year ago at the close in the Cretaceous Period.

Rhynchosaurs

Rhynchosaurs were a highly successful archosauromorph reptile group that existed throughout the Triassic Period. They first appeared in their Olenekian Age of the Early Triassic and then went extinct in their Carnian or Norian Age of the Late Triassic.

Rhynchosaurus was a member of the Anisian Age of the Middle Triassic between 247 million years and about 242 million years in the past:

Rhynchosaurs were herbivores that were is distinguished by its large arms and bodies. Maxilla (the bone that makes up the jaw's upper part) along with the jaw were altered to form tooth plates that were flattened. The hind feet were fitted with claws designed to dig. The first rhyncosaurs were tiny and had bodies resembling lizards. Later species measured up to 2.25 metres (6.5 feet) in length. They also were triangular in their skulls, with powerful jaw muscles and jaws that fit tightly and were perfect for cutting through the tough plant material.

Hyperodapedon (also also known as Scaphonyx) was a rhynchosaur found in late Triassic. Late Triassic:

Allokotosaurs

Allokotosaurs were a species of archosauromorph reptiles which were found during the Middle and Late Triassic. The majority of members were herbivores, but one of them, Pamelaria (see below) is believed to be insectivore. As of now two species of animals are believed to be members of Allokotosauria

These are the Trilophosauridae as well as the Azendohsaurid.

Trilophosaurus buettneri:

The Trilophosauridae were lizardlike in their form. The most well-known of the family is Trilophosaurus which was found within the Late Triassic and was up to 2.5 meters (8.2 feet) in length. Trilophosaurus was a massively built skull and was likely equipped with the beak with horns. The jaws of the animal had large cheek teeth that had sharp edges that were perfect for consuming tough plants.

Trilophosaurus buettneri fossil:

The Azendohsauridae had necks that were long and tiny heads. The most diminutive relatives were 1.5 metres (4.9 feet) long and weighed approximately 40 kilograms (88 pounds). The most powerful family members were four metres (13.1 feet) in length and weighed approximately 200 kilograms (440 lbs). The first Azendohsauridae emerged in the 245 million year period and the most recent relatives of this family were extinct the age of 216 million. Family members comprise Azendohsaurus Malerisaurus, Pamelaria and Shringasaurus.

Azendohsaurus was a species that lived during The Late Triassic Epoch in what is now

Morocco. There are two species of Azendohsaurus that have been identified. The first species that was discovered Azendohsaurus laaroussi is only known by a fragment of jaw that has teeth. Two fossils from Azendohsaurus madagaskensis, the other species Azendohsaurus madagaskensis have been discovered and are more complete enough to show it is with Trilophosaurus.

Malerisaurus is an archosauromorph that measured about 1.2 metres (3.9 feet) in length. It was probably an insectivore. It was identified from Late Triassic fossils found in India and Texas, USA. In 1980, when it was first described, Malerisaurus was initially considered as a protorosaur. However, more recent research conducted in the years 2006 and 2017 suggest it's an allokotosaur. The research conducted in 2006 found that Malerisaurus was just an abbreviation for Trilophosaurus however, the 2017 study determined that Malerisaurus was part of the Azendohsauridae group.

Pamelaria was a native of her time in the Middle Triassic in what is now India. It was approximately two meters (6.6 feet) in length. It was small in its head, long neck and swaying legs that could give the animal an identical posture to Lizards. Pamelaria likely used the tail's base and its limbs to help support its weight. The neck was positioned above the body during life and the animal would be in a position to raise or lower its neck from the base and rotate its neck, however sideways movements would have been limited. The jaws were fitted with tiny conical teeth, and it is believed that Pamelaria was an insectivore. Insect burrows can be found in the same rock formations in the areas where Pamelaria fossils were discovered that is in line with this theory. Pamelaria is recognized from fossils discovered by six individuals at three locations, including one skeleton which is almost complete.

Shringasaurus was between 3 and four metres (9.8 up to 13.1 feet) long . It lived during the Anisian Age of the Middle Triassic Epoch in what is now India. It had two horns that were on their fronts. The skull can be roughly described as rectangular , with conical horns that were short.

The first time they appeared was at early Middle Triassic about 247 million years ago, allokotosaurs went extinct at the end of the Triassic possibly during the Triassic-Jurassic extinct event that occurred 201 million years ago.

Phytosaurs

Phytosaurs were a family of semi-aquatic reptiles which first appeared in the middle of the Triassic Epoch. They all preyed on predators and were typically big reptiles.

Smilosuchus Adamanensis, one of the Late Triassic phytosaur that lived in North America:

The Phytosaurs looked like the current crocodilians in regards to size and appearance, but there were some significant distinctions. They had the ankles being more primitive unlike crocodilians, minus the bony second palate that crocodiles sport nostrils that are above their eyes, rather than on the ends of their snouts, greater armor, and teeth that were serrated, which are better in cutting meat more effectively than the crocodile's.

Brachysuchus megalodon skull:

In the past, phytosaurs had been considered to be early pseudosuchians and were placed within the same category as the crocodiles. Recent research suggests that phytosaurs are Archosauriformes which means they had a close relationship with archosaurs from the beginning, and diverging from them before the crocodile line (Pseudosuchia) and the bird-line (Avemetatarsalia) archosaurs separated. The similarities between phytosaurs and crocodilians could be the result of convergence evolution.

Rutiodon fossil:

Phytosaurs are believed to have gone extinct by the close in the Triassic Period but there is evidence that suggests some species could have survived to The Early Jurassic. The most convincing evidence of phytosaurs that survived past that of the Triassic is the existence of a number of phytosaur teeth within Jurassic rocks found in France. It is also possible that these teeth may have either been misidentified , or have been transferred out of Late Triassic rocks into Early Jurassic deposits. There is also a piece from an upper jaw found in Early Jurassic rocks in China and a second piece from a jaw lower that is from England that could both are Jurassic phytosaurs. It could be there is a possibility that the Chinese jaw is incorrectly identified and that the English jaw is not correctly date.

Phytosaur tooth:

Proterosuchids and Erythrosuchids

The proterosuchids comprised a family consisting of archosaur-like (archosauriform) reptiles that existed throughout the Late Permian and Early Triassic between 252 million years between 247 million years in the past. As we've previously mentioned the extinction event of the Permian Triassic which took place around 252 million years earlier, wiped out nearly 95percent of species, including all of the major therapsid species. This created a number of ecological areas which other species could take advantage of In just 5 million years, proterosuchids underwent an adaptive evolution to become into a variety of carnivores from terrestrial and semi-aquatic species.

The outwardly-facing proterosuchids resembled crocod. They were usually 1.5 metres (4.9 feet) taller, and slimmer than crocodiles and did not have those steel scales (scutes) which crocodiles possess. Their skeletons were more primitive than crocodiles ' and their limbs were shorter, which gave them an expansive posture. Proterosuchids are easily recognized through a slant in the top of their jaw.

Proterosuchus:

The proterosuchids were believed to have led to an archosauriformes group called the erythrosuchids. The erythrosuchids have been found as being closely related to the proterosuchids however not descended from them.

Erthyrosuchids were big predators that had lengths of between 2.5 to five meters (8.2 feet up to 16.4 feet). They had huge skulls and could be easily identified by an "step" across the bones that comprised the lower jaw (the maxilla and the premaxilla). Erthyrosuchids also had an upright posture like archosaurs as well as their fourth trochanter knob that was on their femur.

Aetosaurs

Aetosaurs were heavily armored archosaurs who lived in the Triassic Late Epoch. Their armor was composed of bone plates (osteoderms) protecting the animal's back, sides underneath and tail. The osteoderms are likely to be covered in horns throughout their lives and pitted, then covered with grooves radial on their backs and sides, but they were soft on their belly. A lot of species also had noticeable spikes around their necks and shoulders.

Aetosaurus:

Aetosaurs had heads that were small, upturned nostrils, and limbs that were short and positioned beneath their bodies in a posture known as pillar-erect. They typically had tiny leaf-shaped teeth that were which were suitable for a diet of herbivores However, certain species have modifications to their teeth and their snouts that may have been employed to feed on insects from colonies. Every species seems to have adaptations to digging, like large hind feet equipped with claws as well as a short radius (lower-arm bone) in relation the humerus (upper-arm bone).

Aetosaurus fossil:

The tiniest species of aetosaurs like Aetosaurus as well as Coahomasuchus were between 1 and 1.5 metres (3.3 or 5 feet) in length. Other species, like Typothorax and Paratypothorax also had large bodies, and could reach three metres (9.8 feet) in length. The largest species known Desmatosuchus was the largest known species with an elongated body that increased to 4.5 metres (14.8 feet) in length.

These armored plates are commonly fossilized, and are found in numerous Triassic rocks. Aetosaurs are also known to be widely distributed, however they was only present for a limited time - thus fossils from every species are only found in rocks that have a certain time period (short stratigraphic region). Aetosaurs are therefore able to be used to serve as chronologies (also called indicator fossils or guide fossils) or fossils that are used to determine the geological time that the rocks in a strata date from.

The cast on Aetosaurus armored carapace

Aetosaurs were commonplace throughout The Late Triassic. Their fossils have been discovered on every continent, with the exception of Australia as well as Antarctica. Aetosaurs became extinct around, or shortly before the Triassic-Jurassic extinctive event.

Desmatosuchus:

Revueltosaurus

Revueltosaurus was an archosaur with crocod (more closely connected to crocodiles than dinosaurs or birds) which closely resembled Aetosaurs. They were present within the Late Triassic between about 225 million years between 209 million years prior, in different regions of the present day in the United States including Arizona, New Mexico and North Carolina. There are three types of revueltosaurus are recognized.

Revueltosaurus:

Revueltosaurus measured around 1 meters (3.3 feet) in length. It was known to be an herbivore due its teeth, which were clearly designed to feed on plant matter. The Revueltosaurus was incorrectly identified as being an earlier ornithischian ("bird-hipped") dinosaur because their teeth are remarkably identical. However, today, the Revueltosaurus has been classified as part of Suchia which is one of the crocodile-line archosaurs.

Revueltosaurus skull:

Poposauroids

Poposauroidea is a species of archosaurs with a crocodile line (more closely connected to crocodiles, than dinosaurs or birds) which lived in the Triassic Period. The poposauroids all share the same ancestor and the group comprises an astonishingly diverse collection of reptiles that include those called poposaurids (members from the Poposauridae family - notice the spelling is different) as well as ctenosauriscids, shuvosaurid and several unusual species like Lotosaurus as well as Qianosuchus. Each one of them is described below.

The poposaurids were carnivores of large size archosaurs who lived in the Triassic's late Epoch. Fossils from this group are located throughout North as well as South America. They varied in length from 2.5 to five meters (8.2 feet up 16.4 feet). They resembled to theropods, carnivores in appearance dinosaurs, and had a comparable to a bipedal (walking in two-footed) position. But the similarities between the two groups are the result of convergent evolution and not common ancestral.

The most famous poposaurid was Poposaurus which was around four meters (13 feet) long , and also had a tail that comprised about half of the length of its body. Poposaurus weighed in the range of 60 to 75 kilograms (132 to 165 pounds) However, some were heavier, with a weight of 90-100 kg (200 to 220 lbs).

Poposaurus:

Ctenosauriscids were a different type of poposauroid. They diverged from the other members of Poposauroidea during the Early Triassic. The group was among the first archosaurs to be successful and they spread out through at least six different genera, including Arizonasaurus, Bromsgroveia, Bystrowisuchus, Ctenosauriscus, Hypselorhachis and Xilousuchus. Fossils belonging to the group were found throughout Africa, Asia, Europe and North America, in both Early Triassic and Middle Triassic rocks. Ctenosauriscids are carnivores that were equipped with sharp teeth, and possessed the quadrupedal stance (walked with four feet). The most notable feature of the group was the "sail" on their backs that gave them a superficial similarity to the pelycosaurs with sails of the Permian like

Dimetrodon and the Edaphosaurus (see Before the Dinosaurs).

The shuvosaurids were a family with closely-related poposauroids which existed in the Triassic Late Epoch. The remains of members of this group have been discovered throughout North as well as South America. Shuvosaurids were bipedal, and were lightly armored. Although they were not very closely related to them shvosaurids are very similar to ornithomimid ("bird mimic") dinosaurs from their time in the Late Cretaceous (see Dinosaurs & Other Animals of the Cretaceous). Shuvosaurids are considered to be toothless herbivores.

Lotosaurus was an elongated poposauroid that was found within the Middle Triassic. The fossils of the dinosaur are only known in central China. Lotosaurus was 1.5 up to 2.5 metres (4.9 8.2 to 8.2 feet) in length and was quadrupedal. In contrast to the other sail-backed poposauroids as well as like the ctenosauriscids, Lotosaurus was a herbivore. Actually, despite its exterior distinct characteristics (such as having sails instead of having no sail and being quadrupedal instead of having a bipedal form), Lotosaurus was closely associated with the shuvosaurids and less to other outwardly related ctenosauriscids.

Qianosuchus is a different poposauroid. It was a member of the Middle Triassic in what is now the southern part of China. It is unique in that it was aquatic and adapted to a semi-marine life style. Qianosuchus is the only archosaur of the Triassic who was adapted to this type of life. It had a wide and flat tail, making it proficient in swimming. Qianosuchus likely hunted on land as well as in the water. Most likely, it had a similar lifestyle to those of saltwater crocodiles of today.

Ornithosuchids

Ornithosuchids were another group of archosaurs with a crocodile line. They lived in their time in the Late Triassic and fossils have been discovered in Argentina and in the United Kingdom.

Ornithosuchids were generally quadrupedal, however they could move on both legs during short amounts for a short period of period (facultatively bipedal). They would only move bipedally in situations where they were required to run quickly. Certain scientists have suggested that ornithosuchids are scavengers since it is evident that they ate animal flesh however, they appear to be ill-equipped to hunt live prey.

Rauisuchoids

Rauisuchoidea is an archosaur group that is crocodile-line that lived in the Triassic Period. It is composed of two families: the Rauisuchids (members belonging to the Rauisuchidae family - notice the difference in spelling) along with the prestosuchids (members of the Prestosuchidae family).

Rauisuchoids walked erectly that had their legs directly under their body, however , this group had a distinct type of erect walk than those of, say dinosaurs. In rauisuchoids the hip socket creates an elongated bone shelf to the femur of the animal and is referred to as the pillar-erect posture.

One example of a Rauisuchoid is Postosuchus which was among the apex predators in the Late Triassic. Postosuchus was approximately 4 to five meters (13 -16 feet) in length. It is believed to be bipedal due to the fact that its forelimbs are shorter than its hindlimbs.

Postosuchus kirkpatricki:

The prestosuchids also were apex predators. They were apex predators that ranged between 2.5 up to seven metres (8.2 up to 23 feet).

Prestosuchids appeared to be widespread in the Middle as well as Late Triassic, between about 245 million years between 245 million and about 216 million years earlier. The fossils of their fossils were discovered across Africa, Europe, India and South America.

Rauisuchoids disappeared in the middle of Triassic Period during the Triassic-Jurassic Extinctions event. It is possible that the existence of rauisuchoids restricted the chances of carnivore dinosaurs to eat since, shortly after the rauisuchoids were extinct, the meat-eating dinosaurs grew in dimensions.

Crocodylomorpha

Crocodylomorpha is the family of archosaurs, which includes crocodiles as well as extinct cousins. There is a common misconception that crocodiles aren't drastically altered their appearance in they first appeared in the Triassic Period, but this is not true. It is factual that there were animals that had similar physiques and/or habits to contemporary crocodiles like the phytosaurs as well as Qianosuchus but it is certain that the members of Crocodylomorpha have experienced significant evolution since their first appearance at the time of the Late Triassic about 225 million years ago.

Triassic Crocodylomorphs are all tiny creatures that could move easily on the ground, however, later, crocodylomorphs developed into forms that had a huge variety of physical plans and habits:

* In those Jurassic as well as the Cretaceous periods (see Dinosaurs & Other Animals of the Jurassic and Dinosaurs & Other Animals of the Cretaceous) There were marine species, called thalattosuchians with flippers and tail fins.

* In the time of the Cretaceous (see Dinosaurs & Other Animals of the Cretaceous), there were herbivores on the terrestrial crocodiles like Chimaerasuchus as well as Simosuchus.

* In the Cenozoic Era (see After the Dinosaurs) Terrestrial running (cursorial) Crocodiles, known as the Planocraniidae were found throughout Asia, Europe and North America. It is believed that the Planocraniidae even had legs which ended in sharp claws shaped like hoofs.

* True crocodiles, which are part of today's crocodile species were not discovered until the late Cretaceous epoch. This group was more diverse ecologically than it is now. As an example, a family of the real crocodiles the Mekosuchinae comprised the arboreal (living in trees) species (Mekosuchus inexpectatus) and

was the home of one of Australia's most formidable predators of terrestrial animals, Quinkana. Mekosuchus inexpectatus was extinct four thousand years ago, while Quinkana was probably 40,000 years old at the time of its death.

Hesperosuchus agilisis one of the crocodylomorphs of the Late Triassic:

Dinosaurs and Dinosauromorpha

Dinosaurs, and their most closely related cousins, Dinosauromorpha, are also archosaurs. They are however covered in Chapter 8.

The term "dinosaur" is a reference to "terrible Lizard" was invented by British biologist Sir Richard Owen (July 20th, 1804 to December 18th the year 1892). Owen also established the Natural History Museum in London.

Chapter 8: Dinosaurs And Dinosauromorpha Of The Triassic Period

Dinosaurs comprise a variety of archosaurs which first appeared during the Triassic Period between about 243 million years ago and around 233 millions of years earlier. At first, dinosaurs weren't especially successful, with archosauromorphs and therapsids dominating ecological niches in terrestrial ecosystems. However, by the close in the Triassic Period most of their opponents died, and dinosaurs were their dominant terrestrial animal. They remained this way throughout their Jurassic as well as the Cretaceous Periods. In addition, they are believed to have evolved from theropod dinosaurs in the Jurassic Period, so strictly saying, birds are also dinosaurs.

Non-avian (non-bird) dinosaurs went extinct around the middle of the Cretaceous Period. Birds have remained alive to this day and are extraordinarily varied and successful - there are over 10,000 species of living birds in contrast to only 5 416 living mammals. Another indicator of the longevity of dinosaurs is that fossils from non-avian dinosaurs are able to be discovered on every continent and in the present, the birds (avian dinosaurs) remain on every continent. Furthermore, birds have nearly every habitat available, including marine and terrestrial habitats in addition to non-avian dinosaurs. comprised those from the land (most aren't avians) as well as aquatic species (such like Spinosaurus) as well as certain species that be able to be able to fly and glide (such such as Microraptor).

Spinosaurus was a carnivore dinosaur from the Cretaceous Period:

The definition used by scientists for Dinosauria which is the group of dinosaurs encompasses all species that descend from the most recent common ancestral lineage of Triceratops as well as birds. A variety of alternative definitions have been suggested, such as all animals descendant from the common ancestral ancestor that was Megalosaurus or Iguanodon (two species to be called dinosaurs) however, the alternative definitions do not make any significant difference as they include the same group of animals.

Triceratops was a resident of Triceratops' time during the Late Cretaceous Epoch:

The definition used by scientists to define dinosaurs implies that certain animals that resemble dinosaurs aren't classified as dinosaurs. These are known in the scientific community as Dinosauriformes (which encompasses dinosaurs as well as some of their closely related species) as well as Dinosauromorpha (which encompasses any animal that is closer to dinosaurs, but not Pterosaurs). It is also important to remember that the majority of animals from the prehistoric period, although commonly portrayed in the minds of people as dinosaurs, aren't particularly like dinosaurs and aren't dinosaurs at all. In addition Dimetrodon (see Before the Dinosaurs) along with ichthyosaurs, plesiosaurs (see chapter 6) Mosasaurs, ichthyosaurs (see Dinosaurs & Other Animals of the Cretaceous), and Pterosaurs (see chapter 7) aren't dinosaurs!

Ixalerpeton:

A good instance of an anthropomorphic dinosaur would be Ixalerpeton is an extremely small bipedal species which lived during the Late Triassic Epoch in what is now Brazil. Ixalerpeton is very closely connected to Dinosauriformes and is part of the Lagerpetidae family, which likely shared an ancestor common to the first Dinosauriformes.

Ixalerpeton is located in the same strata of rock as the earlier sauropodomorphs like Buriolestes. Similar to that yet another member from the Lagerpetidae family, Dromomeron, is also located in the same strata with an additional dinosaur Chindesaurus. Therefore, we can conclusively say that the time dinosaurs first appeared they didn't immediately replace dinosauromorphs, but rather existed alongside dinosauromorphs for a long duration of.

Silesaurus was one of the Dinosauriform that was found in the Late Triassic. The skeleton of Silesaurus has many but not all the distinctive characteristics of dinosaurs.

The decision of whether an animal is as a dinosaur or not is determined by its lineage, however there is a way to establish whether the animal is one through examining its bones. It is because each dinosaur shares certain characteristics (synapomorphies) that they inherited from their common predecessors (or in some instances are direct descendants of earlier dinosaurs that have synapomorphies) These characteristics aren't present in other categories. Synapomorphies are characterized by the fact those where there is a region of the radius (lower-arm bone) is always shorter than the 80 percent of the humerus (upper-arm bone) and the fourth trochanter on the femur (thighbone) is an angular flanne. One example of a feature that isn't classified as a synapomorphy is the presence of 2 pairs of temporal fenestrae as the feature is not just in dinosaurs , but throughout diapsids. This includes such things as archosaurs as well as Lepidosauromorpha.

Marasuchus is a Dinosauriform that lived around 223 million years prior to. While it had a few dinosaur-like characteristics however, it didn't have the complete set of dinosaur traits (synamorphies) in addition to having a number of primitive (plesiomorphic) characteristics.

Dinosaurs are traditionally thought of as slow as well as cold blooded (ectothermic) species. Many scientists now think that these were lively creatures that had a high metabolic rate. It is still a topic of inquiry the question of whether dinosaurs that were not avian are cold blooded warmed-blooded (endothermic) or a mix of both.

Evidence of active dinosaurs animal includes:

For all lineages of dinosaurs, at the very least the hindlimbs stand up rather than the sprawling position seen in the majority of reptiles.

* Dinosaurs probably used some sort of mechanism to regulate their temperature, as they thrived within cold environments. It could have been metabolic, but it could also have been insulation feathers or by larger species keeping the heat because of the size of their bodies (mass homeothermy).

The evidence that dinosaurs were endothermic includes the possibility that dinosaurs were able to live in polar areas and the blood vessels found in fossil bones appear to be similar to those found in a typical endotherm. In addition, as birds descend of dinosaurs, it is suggested (with some evidence) that dinosaurs might have had an identical respiratory system, that included air sacs. These air sacs could have enlarged the lungs, which would have allowed more activity than similar-sized mammals, and also allowing big dinosaurs to efficiently chill themselves.

Comparative analysis of air sacs in non-avian dinosaurs (Majungasaurus) as well as in the bird:

Even though all dinosaurs had hind-limbs that were erect however, there was a wide range in body plans and living styles. For instance there were quadrupedal and bipedal dinosaurs. there were herbivorous, carnivorous and omnivorous dinosaurs. Furthermore, there were tiny (chicken-size or smaller) and huge dinosaurs. The most fundamental division of dinosaurs however was dependent on the bones of their hips.

Saurischia and Ornithischia

Scientists have divided dinosaurs into two subdivisions (orders):

* Saurischia - Saurischia (lizard-hipped dinosaurs) retained the hip-shaped structure that was found in earlier reptiles and the hips of this group were anatomically identical to those of the lizards as well as other reptiles of today. Saurischians are usually identified due to their pelvic three-pronged structure and the pubis bone pointed toward the front. The members of Saurischia include dinosaurs (such such as Allosaurus as well as

Tyrannosaurus) and sauropodomorphs (such as Apatosaurus and Brachiosaurus). In the end, as a result of a process of convergence, there are several linesages belonging to theropod subgroup such as therizinosaurs (herbivorous theropods sporting massive claws) as well as Avialans (birds and several of their close relatives) and perhaps the dromaeosaurs (the group which includes Velocirator) independently developed an ornithischian-like hip system (see the next section below). Be aware that despite having ornithischian-like hips, dinosaurs of this era are not considered to be saurischians.

* Ornithischia * Ornithischia Ornithischia (bird-hipped dinosaurs) have their pubic bones moved backwards to form an enlarged pelvic structure with four prongs. The change to this configuration is likely to be due to the necessity to create larger stomachs for herbivorous as well as multi-grain diets. The majority of ornithischians were herbivores. Ornithischians are distinguished from saurischians who have developed hips that resembled ornithischian by a variety of anatomical traits. For example, ornithischians have an additional bone in upper jaws, which is called predentary.

Hip structure in Eoraptor one of the earliest saurischian dinosaur (top) in addition to Lesothosaurus an ornithischian early dinosaur (bottom):

Gi

Saurischians have been the first dinosaur group to be discovered during their time in the Late Triassic Epoch at least about 233 millennia ago. Ornithischians didn't appear until much later. Eocursor (described within the chapter about Early Ornithischian Dinosaurs) is most likely the first known ornithischian however the date is not certain and it's not clear whether it existed during early Late Triassic or Early Jurassic. Another possible candidate for the first ornithischian could be Pisanosaurus. But, even though Pisanosaurus lived within the Late Triassic, it is not clear what it is, and may be an ornithischian dinosaur , or could be an Dinosauriform. Other early ornithischians were belonging to the Heterodontosauridae group (see Dinosaurs & Other Animals of the Jurassic) which's fossils first surface in the early stages in the Jurassic.

Triceratops (an ornithischian from the Cretaceous) skull. The predentary bone is labeled 11.

Early Saurischian Dinosaurs

Staurikosaurus is among the dinosaurs that were discovered in the early days of. It was a member of the Late Triassic Epoch about 233 million years ago. It was a tiny, agile carnivore, about 2.25 metres (7.4 feet) long, around 800 centimeters (2.6 feet) tall and weighed about 30 kilograms (66 lbs).

We know that Staurikosaurus was bipedal, and the fastest runner due to the shape that its legs. We also are aware that its jaws were able to capture and hold prey and cut through flesh since the teeth were serrated and were curved inwards toward the neck. But, a few characteristics of Staurikosaurus remain elusive. It is because we don't yet have an entire fossil. For instance, Staurikosaurus is usually depicted as having five fingers and five toes. This is which is a typical condition in primitive dinosaurs that are not specialized, however we don't know for sure believe that this was the case.

Staurikosaurus:

A close cousin of Staurikosaurus and also living during the Late Triassic was Herrerasaurus. Herrerasaurus was approximately 221,000 years old, and belonged to the same Staurikosaurus clan (the Herrerasauridae family) but was significantly bigger. Similar to Staurikosaurus, Herrerasaurus was a bipedal carnivore, but it could reach up to 6-meters (20 feet) tall and weighed up to 350 kilograms (770 lbs).

Herrerasaurus:

We know that Herrerasaurus was a fast-running animal because it had strong hindlimbs with short thighs, as well as long feet, all of which were adapted to speed. The tail, too, is stiffened by the overlapping projections of vertebrae, and, therefore, clearly designed to stabilize the body when moving at a high speed. The forelimbs on Herrerasaurus are specifically designed to grasp prey. The forearm and the upper arm are both small, however the hands are longer. The thumb and the initial two fingers end in sharp claws that are curved and designed to be used for gripping.

Herrerasaurus also had a unique mixture of advanced, primitive and unusual characteristics. In particular, even though its pelvis is generally similar to the pelvis from saurischian reptiles, its pelvis also has the most primitive as well as advanced features such as the ilium (the principal hip bone) is supported by just two sacrals (a primitive or basal characteristic) however the pubis bone slants in the opposite direction (an advanced or related feature). In the same way, Herrerasaurus had a narrow skull, which resembled the skulls of archosaurs from earlier times (a primitive characteristic) however, it also had an elastic joint in the lower jaw which would aid in grabbing prey (an uncommon feature for a dinosaur, but one that lizards have independently developed).

Herrerasaurus skull:

Another herrerasaurid from The Late Triassic is Chindesaurus. Chindesaurus fossils were discovered in the southwest United States including specimens found in Texas and the Petrified Forest National Park in Arizona.

Chindesaurus was between 2 and 2.3 metres (6.6 feet to 7.5 feet) in length. Its weight isn't known but it was probably less than 50kg (110 pounds). At first by scientists, they believed that it might be an earlier sauropodomorph (see below) However, nowadays the majority of researchers are of the opinion that Chindesaurus was bipedal carnivore, and have assigned this species as belonging to the Herrerasauridae family.

Chindesaurus:

The First Theropods

The Herrerasauridae family was an early, unspecialized saurischian dinosaurs that superficially resembled later theropods. It is not clear whether they are primitive theropods, predate the theropod/sauropodomorph split, or perhaps even predate the saurischian/ornithischian split. The first known definitive theropod is Eoraptor was found during the Late Triassic Epoch between about 231 million years between 228 million years in the past. In the year Eoraptor came to light in the year 1993, it was thought to be the oldest dinosaur ever discovered.

Eoraptor:

Eoraptor was tiny and light constructed. It was just 1 meters (3.3 feet) in length and weighed approximately 10 kilograms (22 lbs).

It was bipedal, and ran in the toes (digitigrade) that were on its hindlimbs. Each forelimb was equipped with five digits. Three of which were capped by claws used to grasp prey, and two of them were merely stubs that were tiny. Eoraptor was home to multiple tooth types (heterodont dentition) with serrated teeth on the jaw's upper side that were used for eating flesh and leaf-shaped tooth on the jaw's lower part, which were suitable to eat plants, which is why scientists believe it consumed an all-omnivorous diet.

Eoraptor lunensis fossil found in the soils of Argentina. The upper and lower limbs and the backbone are visible.

Coelophysis was a second early theropod. It was present within the Late Triassic and Early Jurassic between 21 millions of years old and the era of 196 millions of years earlier. Coelophysis appears to have been widespread because fossils have been discovered throughout southern Africa, the United States as well as in southern Africa.

Coelophysis:

Three varieties of Coelophysis have been identified : Coelophysis bauri Coelophysis

Rhodesiensis and Coelophysis Kayentakatae. Coelophysis was bipedal and thinly constructed. The largest animals could reach up to 3 metres (9.8 feet) in length.

Comparative size of Coelophysis bauri with Coelophysis Rhodesiensis

Coelophysis was a carnivore with a speedy run. Its teeth were sharp and jagged with fine serrations obviously designed to slice through flesh . The forelimbs were perfectly adapted to taking prey. Research suggests that it had sharp vision, perhaps similar to an eagle or any other birds of prey. Coelophysis likely primarily was a hunter of small prey, like lizards, but it may have also hunted in groups to take down larger prey.

Coelophysis:

Footprints of Coelophysis:

Sauropodomorpha

Sauropods were a species of saurischian dinosaurs that were the predominant herbivores in their time, the Jurassic as well as Cretaceous Periods. They were quadrupedal beasts with legs that resembled pillars, long necks, tails that were long, and heads that were relatively small. Sauropods of all kinds grew to massive dimensions, and some were among the biggest terrestrial mammals in the history of Earth. Some of the most well-known sauropods include Apatosaurus, Brachiosaurus, Diplodocus and Supersaurus (which all existed in the Jurassic Period), and Ampelosaurus, Argentinosaurus and Paralititan (which all lived during the Cretaceous Period).

Brachiosaurus size:

The group of sauropods, as well as closely related species as well as their ancestors is known as Sauropodomorpha. Sauropodomorphs first were discovered within their earliest stages in the Late Triassic about 231 million years ago. The early sauropodomorphs generally smaller than the later sauropods, and were usually bipedal.

It has been long thought that the earliest sauropodomorphs are carnivores. This idea gained empirical confirmation with the discovery in the year 2016 of Buriolestes. Buriolestes is an earlier basal sauropodomorph, about 1.3 meters (4.3 feet) long. One of the most notable characteristics of Buriolestes is the fact that it has serrated, curved teeth that were specifically designed to slice flesh.

Buriolestes teeth:

A different early sauropodomorph could have had meat as part of its diet during Panphagia. Panphagia was also present in its Late Triassic about 231 million years in the past. It was a tiny bipedal creature. The exact dimensions are not 100% certain, as it's currently known from one fossil found in 2009. The fossil we have comes taken from a young animal around 1.3 metres (4.3 feet) in length, however the maximum length of an adult was most likely around 1.7 meters (5.6 feet).).

The word Panphagia translates to "eat everything" and is meant as an allusion to the probable diet of the animal. it's believed to be an Omnivore. This is due to the fact that the teeth of Panphagia are intermediate (and believed as transitional) in shape between carnivore dinosaurs and sauropodomorphs that are herbivores. Panphagia includes pointy spearlike (sublanceolate) teeth designed to cut flesh, and the leaf-shaped back teeth that are designed for chewing plants.

Panphagia Dimensions:

A different very primitive and early (basal) sauropodomorph was Saturnalia that lived in the Triassic's Late Epoch around two billion years old. Fossils from Saturnalia were discovered across the two continents of South America and Africa (which were joined during this time). Saturnalia may be linked with the common ancestor of theropods and sauropods since it has many features resembling theropods.

Saturnalia is likely to have been quadrupedal at least a little bit period of time. It could also rear its hindlimbs on its hindlimbs to escape predators bipedally. Saturnalia was around 1.5 metres (5 feet) in length and likely weighed 10 kilograms (22 pounds). Its diet isn't clear however, its skull and hands seem like theropods, which suggests it could have hunted smaller animals and may have hunted down meat in addition to eating plants that later became sauropodomorphs that exclusively ate. Saturnalia is currently identified from only three skeletons , which means there's some uncertainty regarding the dinosaur's diet.

Saturnalia:

One of the basal sauropodomorphs is Thecodontosaurus. Thecodontosaurus was a tiny bipedal herbivore. The fossils found within southern England and is believed to have existed in the latter part in the Triassic between the ages of 204 million and 201 million years ago.

Thecodontosaurus:

More than 200 fossils of Thecodontosaurus have been discovered, though each fragment is a fragment of the entire animal. Furthermore, many fossils, including the one that was used to describe the animal (the kind specimen) and were destroyed due to German bombings throughout World War II. However, with the fragments that are available scientists have been able recreate the entire skeleton the animal, with only the frontal part of the skull.

In an average Thecodontosaurus averaged 1.2 metres (3.9 feet) in length and was about thirty centimeters (1 foot) tall. The largest of them were as high as 2.5 metres (8.2 feet) in length and could be the equivalent of 60 centimeters (2 feet) tall. Thecodontosaurus was a bipedal animal with its forelimbs being smaller than the hindlimbs. It had a relatively small neck, a huge skull, big eyes and a tail which was larger than its neck, head and body.

Thecodontosaurus size:

Although Buriolestes, Panphagia, Saturnalia and Thecodontosaurus were all tiny, Riojasaurus, another sauropodomorph of the Late Triassic, was much bigger. Riojasaurus was 10 metres (33 feet) in length and was alive from 227 to 213 million years old in the region that is now South America.

Riojasaurus had an extended neck, a the long tail as well as a large body. It had strong-built legs and its hind and forelimbs were nearly equal in length. Certain experts consider that Riojasaurus was a quadruped that was obligatory however, some believe it was capable of rearing on its hind limbs, while others believe that it could be bipedal. Based on the structure of the scleral rings (the bone rings that surround the eyes) It has also been proposed it was Riojasaurus could have been cathemeral (also called metaturnal) which implies that the creature was active during short intervals that were evenly spread between day and night.

Riojasaurus:

Melanorosaurus was a sauropodomorph from the Late Triassic. It was found throughout South Africa between about 216 million years ago until the end of the Triassic about 201 million years ago.

Melanorosaurus:

Melanorosaurus was around eight metres (26 feet) in length and weighed about 1.3 tons. It was large in size with strong legs and is believed to be an inherently quadruple.

Melanorosaurus size:

The two Melanorosaurus along with Riojasaurus were herbivores. They according to some researchers, were closely related to one another (although they had some important differences in the neck anatomy). Because of their massive bodies as well as their anatomy of the limbs some scientists believe Melanorosaurus or Riojasaurus might have a close relationship to the early sauropods. Actually, according to certain definitions of sauropods Melanorosaurus could be classified as an animal known as a sauropod.

Another sauropodomorph of herbivores closely with sauropods is Mussaurus. Mussaurus was a member of the Late Triassic between about 215 million years ago and the age of 203 million years in the past. The average size of a mature Mussaurus is approximately six metres (20 feet) in length and weighed approximately 1 tonne.

Mussaurus:

The word Mussaurus refers to "mouse Lizard". The name was chosen because of the small skeletons that were later discovered to be juvenile and infant creatures. We are aware that Mussaurus put out numerous eggs in nests and that the young ones were between 20 and 37 centimeters (7.9 inches to 14.6 inches) in length. It is also believed that in the early years of life Mussaurus was a quadruple, however, as it grew its mass center was moved to the back towards the pelvis, so that by the time it reached adulthood, it was capable of walking bipedally.

The final sauropodomorph species we'll be discussing is Plateosaurus. Plateosaurus was a member of the Late Triassic between about 214 million years ago and around 204 millions of years earlier. Fossils from Plateosaurus have been discovered in northern and central Europe, Greenland, and North America. Fossils (some leg bones and vertebrae) from the animal first surfaced within Germany around 1830 however, since then, many more fossils have been discovered in various locations.

Plateosaurus depicted in a quadrupedal pose (probably impossible physically):

Plateosaurus had a long , flexible neck, and a tiny head with teeth for crushing plants, powerful hindlimbs and short muscular forelimbs that had three fingers with claws to grasp. The adult plateosaurus was between 5 to 10-meters (16 to 30 feet) in length, and likely had a weight of at least 1 tonne.

At the time that Plateosaurus initially was discovered it was not clear what dinosaur group it was part of. It was initially placed within the family of its owner, known as the Plateosauridae however the relation between this family and other groups was not known. The legendary American paleontologist Othniel C. Marsh (October 29th, 1831 until March 18th 19th, 1899) identified Plateosaurus as a theropod by 1895, however, later German scientists Friedrich von Huene (March 22nd 1875 until April 4th April 4th, 1969) put it in the new group known as known as the "Prosauropoda". "Prosauropoda" was described as a category of herbivore dinosaurs that had big bodies with broad feet, large hands, and large skulls, which were likely an ancestor of sauropods. The majority of scientists today do not approve of the the word "Prosauropoda" since they do not believe it to be to be a monophyletic species (containing all descendants of an ancestor with a common ancestral lineage). This is evident by the quotation marks surrounding the phrase "Prosauropoda". Today, rather than using the term prosauropod to describe it, Plateosaurus is often called the basal sauropodomorph.

The posture and movements of Plateosaurus has been the topic of debate among scientists:

* Friedrich von Huene thought the animal was bipedal, and ran with its toes (digitigrade) of the hind limbs.

* A second paleontologist researching the animal around the same timeframe, Otto Max Johannes Jaekel (February 21st, 1863 until

March 6th 1929) believed that the animal was walking quadrupedally an lizard-like position, with its metatarsals and toes lying flat upon the floor (plantigrade).

* One year later, Jaekel made a change of mind and is now suggesting Plateosaurus could have hopped around like the kangaroo!

* In the early 1980s, a majority of researchers were of the opinion that Plateosaurus had limbs that were straight with a digitigrade posture, and that it maintained its back in a horizontal position. It was believed that Plateosaurus was quadrupedal when moving slow and bipedally when moving fast.

The year 2007 saw a thorough examination of the forelimbs of the animal revealed that several skeletons had been improperly assembled by adjusting the positions of the ulna and radius bones forearms swapped. Once the forearm bones had been correctly placed, it was obvious it was evident that Plateosaurus was an obligatory biped.

Plateosaurus seen in a bipedal pose:

Like Riojasaurus Based on the structure of its scleral ring (the bones that surround the eyes) It has been proposed the possibility that

Plateosaurus was cathemeral. That means the animal was in active for brief intervals evenly spread between day and night. It could be that it embraced this way of life to escape the scorching heat of the middle of the day.

Plateosaurus longiceps skeleton:

Early Ornithischian Dinosaurs

The oldest-known ornithischian dinosaur has been identified as Eocursor. It is not clear exactly when it was discovered. Eocursor is still a topic of debate among scientists. However, it may be as old as 210 million and is located within the Triassic Late Epoch. Others think it is more likely that Eocursor is much older and was alive during the Early Jurassic, possibly in the Sinemurian Age, which would indicate that it is less than the age of 199 million.

Eocursor was a tiny, lightly built bipedal dinosaur, about 1 meters (3.3 feet) long. It was a quick running animal with triangular teeth that resembled an omnivorous diet that included animals and plants.

Size of the Eocursor:

Chapter 9: The Triassic Coal Gap

Coal is a brown-black , sedimentary rock used as a fossil fuel , as and in various industrial processes, including steel and iron production. It is composed mainly of carbon, however it also contains other elements in different quantities, mainly oxygen, nitrogen, hydrogen and sulfur. The process of coal formation occurs by the process of removing dead plant material transformed to peat (typically in swamps and bogs) and then converted over millions of years using the pressure and heat into coal.

Coal:

Most often, it is connected to the Carboniferous Period which was a time period that spanned 359 million years between 299 million year ago (the term Carboniferous comes from Latin meaning "coal-bearing") coal can be found in the rocks of all geological times. However coal deposits are rare found in Early as well as Middle Triassic rocks: no coal deposits are found in Early Triassic strata, and coal deposits found in Middle Triassic rock are rare and are thin.

A variety of possible explanations for the different explanations for this coal shortage have been suggested. They include:

* New species of fungi and arthropods, insects and vertebrates developed in the Early Triassic. These species could have killed large numbers forests and even prevented coal developing.

* Factors that are not directly caused through living organisms (abiotic factors) for example, the reduction in rainfall may be the cause of that coal gap.

* Plants that form peat may be extinct during the time of the Permian-Triassic extinction. It is believed that it took about 10 million years other plants to adjust to the acidic and moist conditions in peat Bogs.

This apparent gap in coal might be a result of modifications in the record of sediment. For instance, peat-producing ecosystems might have moved because of changes in climate and have relocated to areas where there is no record of sedimentary evidence. The fact that certain coal deposits found in Antarctica as well as Australia disappear before the

Permian Triassic boundary is in line with this idea.

Chapter 10: Distinction Events That Occurred During The Triassic Period

It is believed that the Triassic Period is situated between two of largest mass extinctions that have occurred in Earth's past: the Permian-Triassic extinctive event (also called the P-Tr extinct as well as the P-T Extinction as well as the End-Permian Extinction, and the Great Dying), and the Triassic-Jurassic Extinction event. In addition, two events of extinction took place during the Triassic The Smith-Spathian extinction and the Carnian Pluvial Event (CPE).

Permian-Triassic Extinction Event

The Permian-Triassic extinction took place near the end of Permian Period shortly before the beginning of the Triassic around 250 million years back. It was the most devastating mass extinction that has ever occurred on Earth and killed 90 to 95% of marine species, and about 70 percent of terrestrial creatures. It affected numerous species and groups that been dominant in throughout the Paleozoic Era, such as the entire extent species of trilobites and trilobites, eurypterids (sea scorpions) as well as a variety of ammonoids, as well as other marine invertebrates. It also affected the majority of parareptiles and the majority of labyrinthodont sauropsid, and therapsid species. The plants were also affected as was the significant shift in the flora of plants due to the eruption. It was also the first mass extinction on Earth's record that impacted insects - this is a sign of the extreme magnitude.

Activity in the Volcanic Zone of Western Siberia (the Siberian Traps) is the most frequently suggested cause of the Triassic-Permian extinctive event. The boundaries of the Siberian traps are represented by the dotted lines on the map. The red and green areas indicate the places where basalt and tuff (both Igneous rocks that resulted from eruptions of volcanic activity) are located:

There are numerous theories concerning the cause or reasons for the Permian-Triassic extinction. This includes:

* Volcanism - One the biggest volcanic events that occurred since the beginning of multicellular life was in the middle of Permian. In a series eruption which lasted for around 2 million years, massive amounts of lava covered vast portions of Siberia in what is

now known as the flood basalt eruption. It is believed that the Siberian Traps, as the area is now referred to is more than 2,000,000 square kilometers (770,000 acres). The eruptions would have generated dust clouds which would have blocked sunlight, interfering with photosynthesis on the oceans and on the land, and creating food chains that would collapse. The other effects of the chemicals released by the eruptions could be acid rain, which caused the death of animals and plants directly, and an increase of atmospheric CO_2 levels and consequently global warming. Certain scientists believe the eruptions may have penetrated carbonate rocks in which coal seams were being formed which could have caused additional carbon dioxide release to the air.

* Frozen methane - If the volcanic activity directly caused higher levels of greenhouse gases and carbon dioxide in the atmosphere, it's possible that it caused a chain of events which increased the temperature even more. If the initial warming caused by volcanism caused the methane reservoirs frozen in the bottom of oceans to melt it could be a significant addition of methane (which is a

potent greenhouse gas) to the atmosphere, and added to the warming.

* Anoxia, Osinia and hypercapnia. There is convincing proof of the existence for the presence of anoxia (low amounts of oxygen) as well as the euxinia (the presence of toxic hydrogen sulfur) as well as hypercapnia (high levels of carbon dioxide) in the Late Permian oceans. Together, they would have killed a variety of marine life. Hydrogen sulfur could have also released into the atmosphere. The changes that occurred in the oceans could have been at first caused by eruptions that occurred in the Siberian Traps but after they began, they could have developed into an self-sustaining feedback loop For instance, anoxia in the oceans may have facilitated the growth of the green sulfur bacteria, which released hydrogen sulfide, and increased the anoxia even more.

* Hydrogen sulfide found in the atmosphere In the event that oceans are rich in hydrogen sulfide, then the gas would also have made it's way to the air. Hydrogen sulfide poisons animals and plants, but more importantly, hydrogen sulfide can also cause damage to

the ozone layer, which would expose the Earth's surface to a devastating amounts of UV radiation.

* Methane producing microbes believed that Methanosarcina is a species of archaea that developed the capacity to process Acetate in the present. By interacting with the stored organic carbon found in the marine sediments of these organisms could release massive quantities of methane and carbon dioxide in the atmosphere which could have caused oxygen depletion in oceans, and an increase in temperature of the entire planet. In the same way, eruptions of the volcanic Siberian Traps released Nickel into the Biosphere and attracting these microbessince nickel is essential to facilitate this process of metabolism.

* Impact event - A meteorite's impact could have caused or contributed to the extinct. The impact could cause huge dust clouds across the sky blocking the Sun and preventing plants from developing. Furthermore, a massive impact could create volcanic activity and all the negative consequences on living things. Some scientists claim that they have discovered evidence from geology within

Australia and Antarctica that suggest an impact occurring at the moment however, other scientists disagree with the claims. The only definitive proof is finding a crater of impact. But any oceanic crater could be long ago erased by the processes of geology. Some locations suggested as potential sites for impact are some of them: the Wilkes Land crater in East Antarctica and a location close to the Falkland Islands and the Araguainha crater located in Brazil. The two sites are not yet time-stamped to know if they are linked to the Triassic-Permian extinction and the Araguainha crater is too small to be responsible for massive mass extinction, despite the fact that the impact may have released and ignited massive quantities of gas and oil.

The supernova star nearby might have exploded in the form of a supernova. The explosion could have created the gamma-ray burst (GRB) which would have killed organisms directly and harm the ozone layer of Earth. While it is plausible, this idea is only speculation as we don't have any evidence that suggests this is actually happening.

The galactic spiral arm is a source of dust Another possibility is that it is possible that the Solar System passed through part of the spiral arm of the Milky way with large quantities of dust. The dust could have diminished light that fell onto the Earth and resulted in an glacial age. This theory is more speculation-based than the supernova hypothesis especially because there isn't any geological evidence that suggests that the ice age was present in the present time.

The Araguainha crater located in Brazil seems to be around the right age , but it seems too small to be responsible for an enormous mass extinction

The majority of scientists will probably believe that the Permian-Triassic extinction occurred by a combination of these causes however, they may differ about the precise cause. It is also believed that geography was a factor during the time of the extinction all of Earth's landmasses joined in a massive supercontinent called Pangaea which means that there was a tiny amount of coastal habitats, which could make marine species more prone to the possibility of extinctions. In addition an additional mass extinction

(Olson's extinct) was in the process of occurring a few million years before and it could have heightened the vulnerability of Earth's ecosystems, which could have increased the impact of the Permian-Triassic extinction it did occur.

Smith-Spathian Extinction Event

In the world of Early Triassic was extremely harsh and devoid of any kind of life. A lot of species had gone extinct, and new species were not yet developed to take their place. Yet, in this state the possibility of another catastrophe arose.

Around two million years ago which is approximately 3 million years following the Permian-Triassic extinctive event, another extinction event took place. This event is referred to as the Smith-Spathian Extinction Event and was triggered by the rise in temperatures. When temperatures in the tropical regions were as high as 40degC (104degF) The large and mobile animals vanished from equatorial and tropical areas in addition to a variety of smaller and less mobile species were killed out. It took around 2 million years for temperatures to drop to normal levels and then only later did animals and plants return to the tropical regions.

As a large number of species already been killed in the Triassic-Permian event The disappearance of a few more species in Smith-Spathian is difficult to determine from the fossil records. Scientists were able to identify the Smith-Spathian through the disappearance of conodonts (extinct teethed jawless fish that resemble Eels) as well as the loss of half the bivalve mollusks from the tropical regions.

Carnian Pluvial Event

It is believed that the Carnian Pluvial event was a climate change event that took place in the Triassic Late Epoch about 300 millennia ago. It was Late Triassic climate was generally dry, however there is ample evidence of greater rainfall and more humid conditions during this time however with dry intervals between them.

The evidence for increased rain is:

* The formation of soils that are influenced by the tropical humid climate.

* Dust assemblages indicate plants that are adapted to the humid climate.

135

* Evidence of an increase in runoff and weathering of rocks due to more rainfall.

* The frequent presence of amber is also a sign that the environment is humid.

Alongside the evidence that suggests an increase in rainfall, there's also evidence suggesting that global warming is taking place of 3 degC (5degF) up to 4degC (7degF). Global warming might be responsible for the increase in rainfall, and may have been caused due to volcanic activity.

If volcanic activity caused the global temperature, then it likely took place in the Wrangellia Igneous Province, which currently is located in southern-central Alaska along with British Columbia. The flood basalt eruption occurred that caused the release of large quantities of CO_2 to the atmosphere, and the subsequent global warming.

Another explanation for the higher rainfall could be caused by the rising from the Cimmerian Orogen. The Cimmerian Orogen is located in areas in central Asia like Turkey, Iran and parts of Tibet. At the time of the Triassic Period, the Cimmerian Orogen was a brand new high mountain range located on the southern part of Laurasia that could have brought monsoon conditions, similar to what the Himalayas in Asia in the present.

Whatever the cause, aside of its impact on climate change, it was also a major cause of climate change. Carnian Pluvial Event also caused major changes in the biological community. Conodonts, bryozoans crinoids, green algae and conodonts all witnessed increased rates of extinct. Following that Carnian Pluvial Event, several major radiations took place, including those among corals, coniferous trees dinosaurs, lepidosaurs and corals.

Triassic-Jurassic Extinction Event

The Triassic-Jurassic extinctive event took place near the end of Triassic Period just prior to the beginning of Jurassic Period, about 201 million years ago. While not as serious as the Permian-Triassic extinction however, it was nonetheless very severe and is believed to be one of the five mass extinction events during the Phanerozoic Eon.

The Triassic-Jurassic extinctions impacted the plants as well as terrestrial and marine animals.

* In the oceans the Triassic-Jurassic extinction destroyed all conodonts and possibly one-third of marine groups (genera) however, fish weren't affected. A statistical analysis has revealed that there was a noticeable reduction in the number of the ray-finned fish (actinopterygians) during the Late Triassic, but it isn't clear whether this is a real consequence or simply caused by sampling bias and, if it is the case the reason behind it. In addition, the only reptile families that went extinct close to the end of Triassic were the only remaining group of plaodonts (the Plascochelyids) and the huge ichthyosaurs (the shonisaurids as well as the shastasaurids).

In the land environment, therapsids as well as a number of large amphibians (temnospondyls) have died however, perhaps the most difficult to hit section was that of the archosaurs, and their archosauro. As we've seen, in the Triassic Period, there was an variety of archosaurs and their archosaur-relatives which filled many of the terrestrial niches. A lot of these groups perished out in the Triassic-Jurassic extinctive event and the only survivors were dinosaurs, pterosaurs, and crocodylomorph.

The most common interpretation of the Triassic-Jurassic Extinction incident has it that the event was brought about by, or was preceded by an ongoing change in the environment. There is evidence to suggest that the planet became more dry around this time and that sea levels fell in the Late Triassic, only to rise again in Early Jurassic. In addition, the climate appears to have changed to be more seasonal, with prolonged periods of drought, sometimes followed by intense monsoons.

But, there is evidence that suggests that the event was swift, possibly happening in as short 10 years. Although it is possible an climatic tipping point may be reached, which would have resulted in sudden and rapid declines in biodiversity, it's also is possible that the extinction event was due to a, catastrophic event like an impact of a meteorite or eruption of volcanic material.

There is now a good amount of evidence that suggests that the event that killed off non-avian dinosaurs is the Cretaceous-Paleogene event is most likely caused by the massive impact of a meteorite (see Dinosaurs & Other Animals of the Cretaceous). Therefore, it is reasonable to examine whether mass extinctions elsewhere throughout the history of Earth could also be the result of impacts.

An impact crater is located located in Canada which is it's the Manicouagan Reservoir in Quebec, that was thought to be a possible likely site for an impact that could be the cause of the Triassic-Jurassic extinction event. This Manicouagan Reservoir is 100 kilometers (62 miles) in size and is a sign of a massive impact to trigger massive extinction. It has since been found to be dated at the year 214 million which suggests it may not be the cause of the Triassic-Jurassic Extinction event.

Other sites of potential impact which have been discovered could be those of the Rochechouart Crater in France and the Puchezh-Katunki crater in Russia and in the

Saint Martin crater in Manitoba, Canada, the Obolon' Krater in Ukraine as well as The Red Wing Creek structure in North Dakota, USA. The Rochechouart is the correct date, but it is just 25 km (16 miles) across, which makes it appear to be too small to be responsible for an extinction mass. The other craters, excluding possibly Puchezh-Katunki, are to be small, and, in any event, require a date to ensure that they're in the right time frame.

The Manicouagan Reservoir in Quebec, Canada:

The evidence that supports the volcanic nature of the Triassic-Jurassic extinctive event lies in the presence of CAMP. Central Atlantic magmatic province (CAMP). With an area of 11,000,000 square kilometers (4,200,000 acres) it is it is Central Atlantic magmatic province is the largest igneous region in the continental continent in the world We know that it was formed in one of the many eruptions of lava that occurred in the Earth's geological past. It is linked to the disintegration of Pangaea and the remains of that events can be seen throughout

North as well as South America, Africa and Europe.

It is believed that the Central Atlantic magmatic province is thought to have formed during a flood basalt eruption about 200 million years back. This naturally coincides with conclusion in the Triassic Period. The eruptions of the volcano may have released carbon dioxide (causing global warming) or sulfur particulates and sulfur dioxide (causing worldwide cooling). There is evidence from geology of an increase in atmospheric carbon dioxide levels at different intervals, which coincide with eruptions that were active which is why the theory of global warming is generally favoured. Additionally, extreme global warming could cause methane reservoirs frozen on deep ocean floors to melt which could have led to an additional warming.

The close relationship between the dates of the eruptions that first began and the beginning of both terrestrial and marine extinctions is an extremely convincing evidence that volcanism was a factor in the

Triassic-Jurassic extinctions. Certain scientists were hesitant to accept the theory of volcanism because the Newark Supergroup that consists of outcrops of rock in the eastern region of the United States, appeared to indicate that the eruptions began at the time in the boundary between Triassic and Jurassic. But, new research and updated dating protocols have established that the majority (but but not every) eruptions of volcanic origin occurred prior to the Triassic-Jurassic border.

The Outcrops from the Newark Supergroup:

Chapter 11: After The Triassic

As we've explained in the previous chapter, we have described that the Mesozoic Era, the period when dinosaurs that were not avian were roaming the Earth is split into three periods: Triassic Period, the Jurassic Period along with the Cretaceous Period. This book will deal only this first three periods, the Triassic Period.

The Jurassic Period

The Jurassic Period is the period of the Mesozoic following the Triassic and spans that began about 201 million years ago until 140 million years ago. The Jurassic witnessed the development of many of the well-known dinosaurs, including Allosaurus, Stegosaurus and Iguanodon and the sauropods such as Apatosaurus, Brachiosaurus and Diplodocus as well as many more species apart from. First birds, geckos, skinks, and sea-going marine crocodiles (thalattosuchians) were also discovered during the Jurassic.

Sauropod dinosaurs first came into existence in early Jurassic Period:

Learn more on this period in the Jurassic Period in my book, Dinosaurs & Other Animals of the Jurassic.

The Cretaceous Period

The final and third period that was part of the Mesozoic Era is called the Cretaceous Period, which spans the time period of around 145 million years ago until the age of 66 millennia ago. In the Cretaceous several new dinosaurs emerged which included Tyrannosaurus Rex (probably the most well-known among all dinosaurs) and the armored and heavily armored Ankylosaurus the duck-billed dinosaurs, as well as the giant ceratopsian dinosaurs, such as Centrosaurus, Styracosaurus and Triceratops. The Cretaceous also witnessed the first appearance of blooming plant (angiosperms) as well in the first "true snakes" Mosasaurs, mosasaurs, and much more.

Ankylosaurus was one the last dinosaurs not avian.

In the middle in the Cretaceous Period, a mass extincture occurred. It is referred to as the Cretaceous Paleogene (K-Pg) the extinction event, or Cretaceous Tertiary (K-T) the extinction event. Numerous animals and plants died out in this massive extinction event, including all non-avian (non-bird) dinosaurs, as well as many other species besides. For a long time, the causes of this mass extinction was the topic of heated discussion among scientists, but there is now a strong evidence that it was brought on by a huge meteorite that struck Earth.

The Cretaceous-Paleogene extinctive event was likely to have been triggered by a huge meteorite strike:

You can learn details information about and the Cretaceous Period in my book Dinosaurs & Other Animals of the Cretaceous.

The Cenozoic Era

Following that Mesozoic Era has ended, the following period is called one of Cenozoic Era which spans the period of 666 million years ago until today. In the Cenozoic the new species emerged mammals, which were earlier small animals became large in size and were able to fill many areas that were previously used by dinosaurs.

Andrewsarchus was a big predator that existed during the Eocene in the early portion of Cenozoic Era:

As with similar to Paleozoic as well as Mesozoic Eras like the Mesozoic and Paleozoic Eras, the Cenozoic Era is divided into periods. For the Cenozoic period, the following are:

* Paleogene Period - The Paleogene Period (also called Palaeogene Period or Palaeogene Period) covers the time period of 66 million years ago until 23 million years in the past. The Paleogene is divided into three periods: Paleocene (also spelled Palaeocene or Palaeocene), Eocene, and Oligocene.

* Neogene Period - The Neogene Period covers the time period of 23 million years back until 2.6 millions of years earlier. The Neogene is divided into two epochs, that of the Miocene along with the Pliocene.

* Quaternary Period - The Quaternary Period covers the time that runs from 2.6

millennia ago until today. It is divided into two periods: that of the Pleistocene along with the Holocene.

The fauna of North America during the Miocene:

To learn more about the what life was like of Earth in the Cenozoic Era, you can refer to my previous book, After the Dinosaurs.

Chapter 12: Dinosaurs

The majority of dinosaurs lived in the soil where vegetation and animal prey are abundant so they're easy to pass by. The following dinosaurs live 100 percent of their time on the ground and lack the ability to fly, glide, or swim.

3.1. PARASAUROLOPHUS

How to Pronounce: Par-ah-sawr-ol-uh-fus

Meaning of the name: Crested Lizard

Weight: 2,500 kilograms

Height 23 feet

Length 31 feet

Life: North America; Alberta, Canada and Utah and New Mexico

Time lived: Cretaceous Period (76 - 7 millions of years ago)

Diet: Herbivore

The Parasaurolophus isn't incredibly swiftly and didn't possess sharp teeth, claws , or any kind of armor. What makes Parasaurolophus so adept in surviving prey is the ability it has to sense enemies approaching from distant. It then alerts its herdmates so that they could move to safe haven. The Parasaurolophus is easy to distinguish different from other dinosaurs due to of the head's shape. It had a curving crest in the area where the nasal cavity was.

The nasal cavity can be described as the tube of one's nose. the Parasaurolophus nasal cavity is quite long, with a length of 8 feet. It's located inside the looping tube, instead of a normal nose. The looping tube is used to the Parasaurolophus to produce a loud sound to alert predators. Its sound can be so powerful that it's more powerful than that of the foghorn. Another characteristic that was the property of Parasaurolophus was the ability to walk on four feet and also walk on two legs similar to apes of are today. It was unable to climb trees, but it ate Cretaceous plants such as ferns or conifers. It was most likely to have was among forests in which plants similar to these thrived.

3.2. OVIRATOR

Pronunciation: O-vih-rap-tore

Meaning of the name Egg Thief

Weight 35 kg

Height 3 feet

Length 7 feet

Lived: Mongolia, China

Time lived: Late Cretaceous Period (70 - 80 million years ago)

Diet: Omnivore

Oviraptor was known as "egg the thief" because the first evidence that was of this kind was discovered on the top of eggs from another dinosaur. Oviraptor was a bird-like creature however it was one of the rare dinosaurs that resembled birds that was found on land. Its feathered hands as well as its small wings weren't ideal to fly.

Oviraptor had a flexible "s" neck with a curved shape, a long tail, shorter arms, and long fingers. The tail was strong and flexible, and has multicolored feathers at the ends. Researchers think that the Oviraptor likely employed its tail to lure female Ovirators. The legs of the animal were slender and long, and were able to run at a high speed and possibly as quick as an Ostrich. Oviraptors consumed small animals such as fruits, insects, seeds and eggs.

3.3. TROODON

How to Pronounce: Gy-ga-noh-teh-sore-uss

Meaning of Name Meaning of Name: Giant Wounding Tooth

Weight 50kg

Size: 6.5 feet

Length 6 feet

Lived: Wyoming, Montana, Alberta; Canada

Time lived: Cretaceous Period (77 million years ago)

Diet: Carnivore

A Troodon is about the same height as the average human. If it was standing upright, it would stand even more taller, but it walks with its head leaning toward the forward, similar to birds. It walked on two feet with claws in with the shape of sickles and teeth that resembled saws. Its arms can be rotated and its hands were three fingers, with sickle-shaped claws.

Troodon was a skilled hunter, and had a large brain due to its size. This makes it the most intelligent dinosaur that has been discovered to date in the present. Troodon was a smart hunter. Troodon was also the one with highest vision of dinosaurs. its eyes were oriented forward and were massive. It allowed them to see prey from a distance and also be able to see at night. It was a big lizard eater and numerous smaller animals and was likely to have resided in the desert plains.

4. THE GROUP OF DINOSAURS

Apart from the two major groups that dinosaurs are divided into, there are four sub-groups in which each species belongs to.

There are many kinds of dinosaurs. There are those who walked on two legs as chickens, as well as ones that have four legs as elephants do. There are some that can swim underwater as well as walk across land as turtles, while others make flights or rest upon branches as Eagles. The majority of prehistoric dinosaurs had armored plates that included horns, scales spikes and even crests. Certain dinosaurs had bumpy, tough skin, similar to the elephants and rhinos.

To properly classify these dinosaurs scientists make use of two main groups as well as 4 sub-groups.

The two main groups of DINOSAURS

Scientists classify dinosaurs into two major categories based on what their waist or pelvic bones look. There are two types of dinosaurs: Saurischia and Ornithiscia.

Saurischia

Saurischia are dinosaurs with hips that look the same as Lizards'. The majority of the top hunter dinosaurs belong to this group.

Ornithiscia

Ornithiscia are dinosaurs with hips as similar as those of birds.. They have beaks, and are predominantly herbivores. Dinosaurs belonging to this group tend to be armored, horned, and have mouths that have duck-billed teeth. They also belong to herds or packs unlike the dinosaurs in the Saurischia group.

The 4 SUB-GROUPS OF DINOSAURS

In addition to being either an Ornithiscia or Saurischia There are four more types that dinosaurs can be divided into. They are Theropod, Sauropod, Cerapod and Theophora.

Theropods

Theropod actually refers to "beast foot" and they are the most frightening dinosaurs to ever be found. Theropods have 2 legs, and they are carnivores that means they consume only meat and do not eat plants or fruits. They are Tyrannosaurus Rex, Velociraptor and Spinosaurus are all part of this class of dinosaur.

Sauropods

Sauropods are able to walk on the four legs of a dinosaur and can be larger over other dinos. Contrary to Theropods Sauropods are herbivores that is, they are only plant eaters. The massive Brachiosaurus and Brontosaurus are part of this kind of dinosaur.

Cerapods

Cerapods comprise dinosaurs that are fascinating due to their appearance. The majority of the dinosaurs from this category sport skulls with helmets such as those of the Triceratops as well as the Parasaurolophus. They're not armored, however they compensate for it by speed or the use of their "helmets".

Thyeophora

Thyeophora is a Latin word meaning "Shield Bearer" and the dinosaurs in this category have armored dinosaurs. Thyeophora dinosaurs generally feature heavy scaled backs or skins, and a majority of them also have spikes. They include the Stegosaurus along with the Ankylosaurus are fantastic examples of theophora dinos.

5. WATER DINOSAURS

Some dinosaurs were not the land. Certain dinosaurs could swim and spend time in water. However, this doesn't mean that they reside in water. They're more similar to Crocodiles which swim, but also make eggs in land, and they spend their time both in water and on land.

5.1. MEOSAURUS

Pronunciation: Meh-zowe-sore -uss

What is the meaning of name? Middle Reptile

Length 3 feet

Diet: Carnivore

Life in: South Africa and South America

Time lived: Early Permian Period (299 - 271 million years ago)

Mesosaurus was a tiny animal with a length of just 3 feet and very skinny. Its feet were like flippers , which could propel its body through the water. It was a huge fan of seafood, fish, and creatures smaller than it. Mesosaurus was a bit like the Gharial or a crocodile renowned for its small and extremely long snout.

Mesosaurus's snout was thick and extremely thin similar to the Gharial Crocodile's. The crocodile had teeth that were sharp inside its mouth, and was known to use it to snap at prey. Its body also resembled an alligator's body, with its long tail and web-like feet. It spent more of its time in the water , rather than on land, and was close to the ocean. The scientists believe Mesosaurus could cover an entire ocean.

5.2. SPINOSAURUS

How to pronounce: Spy-nuh-sore

The meaning behind the name: Spine Lizard

Weight 6350 kg

Height 14 feet

Length 40 feet

Living: North Africa, Egypt, Morocco

Time was lived: Late Cretaceous Period (112 to 97 million years ago)

Diet: Carnivore

Spinosaurus is known as the spine lizard for the stunning sail-like fin that is on its back comprised by its spinal column. The bones supporting the sail-like fin measured about 6 feet long. Spinosaurus Spinosaurus is 20 percent larger that Tyrannosaurus Rex.

Tyrannosaurus Rex and was also likely to be more frightening.

It had a six-foot long head, with a face like a crocodile's as well as an array of sharp straight teeth. This is unique since carnivores all have curved teeth however, the straight teeth aid to allow the Spinosaurus in its ability to consume sea creatures that are slippery. The Spinosaurus loved to swim and most likely, spent longer in the ocean than on land. However, it was known to put eggs onto land. It was primarily a fish eater, but could also consume terrestrial animals when they was found to be hungry on land.

The Spinosaurus was a sea-going creature and, when it hunts on land it is a resident of mangrove forests.

6. Air Dinosaurs

6.1. PTERANADON

What to pronounce: Tear-ann-owe

Meaning of Name The meaning of the name is: No Teeth

Weight 18 kilograms

Length 30 feet

Living: North America, England

Time lived: Late Cretaceous Period (85 - 75 million years ago)

Diet: Carnivore (Seafood)

Pteranodon is a huge reptile that lived close to the ocean, and was a seafood eater to supplement its diet. It was a fan of squid, fish, and the majority of species that were found within the sea. It had a large set of wings that were up to 35 feet wide in length, from one end to the other. It was as wide as hang gliders today. Pteranodon had a massive head rest with a long length as well as a long beak likely for aiding in maintaining balance when flying. It was found in valleys in which there were hills and rivers. This was perfect for it as it was able to fly down to take a drink or feed.

6.2. ICAROSAURUS

Pronunciation: Ik-ahroe-soreuss

Name Meaning: Icarus Reptile

Länge: 1.3 feet

The places where he lived: North America, Utah, Montana, New Jersey

Time was alive: Triassic Period (175 to 200 million years ago)

Diet Herbivore (Insects and small animals)

Icarosaurus was a bit like an lizard, with large wings, and longand thin tail. It was a tiny reptile, and it ate only insects and smaller animals than it. Icarosaurus could not fly, it used its wings to travel long distances. The wings of the dinosaur were not actually wings, but rather membranes with extremely thin bones. The membranes were similar to thin skin. The bone was not linked to the skeleton of Icarosaurus and behaved more like the body of a glider. It was found in subtropical and tropical areas.

6.3. QUETZALCOATLUS

How to Pronounce: Kett zal-coe-atluss

Significance of the Name Mexican Feathered God

Width 100 kg

Length 45 feet

Life: North America, Texas

Time was lived: Cretaceous Period (65 million years ago)

The diet: Herbivore (Fish and Dead Animals)

Quetzalcoatlus is among the biggest flying dinosaurs that has yet to be found as of the present. Its wings were huge that measured up to 40 feet from tip to tip. The Quetzalcoatlus was very large in its neck. It was 10 feet long, and its beak was slender and long too. The scientists believe that Quetzalcoatlus is a known scavenger that took dead animals in order for leftover food. It also consumed fish when taking a scavenge.

7. DINOSAURS with ARMOR

7.1. ANKYLOSAURUS

How to Pronounce: Ann-kisore-uss

Meaning of Name The meaning of the name is: Reptiles that are fused Reptile

Weight 4000 kg

Width, Length and Height 8 feet wide tall, 3-6 feet high and 35 feet long

Lived: North America, Montana

Time lived: Late Cretaceous Period (74 to 65 million years ago)

Diet: Herbivore

Ankylosauria, a category of armored dinosaurs is named for Ankylosaurus, the dinosaur. Ankylososaurus is famous for its armor, and is considered to be one of the few armored dinosaurs that lived. It was able to walk on four legs and had a thick plated back that looked like an armoured armadillo's. The difference was that it was much bigger and packed with spikes.

The spikes were not only located on the back, but also along the sides. Ankylosaurus was a tranquil herbivore and was protected from predators thanks to its armor. Not only was it well protected, Ankylosaurus also had its own weapon for protection. The tip of the tail, there was a type of mace which could deal fatal hits. The mace was as large as 45 pounds and employed to hit the legs of foes. Ankylosaurus is the most secure dinosaur ever discovered. Even its eyes were plated.

7.2. MINMI

How to Pronounce: Minmee

Name Meaning The location on which it was first discovered

Weight 500 kilograms

Length 10 feet

Living: Queensland, Australia

Time was lived: Cretaceous Period (119- the year 113 million)

Diet: Herbivore

Minmi is among the rare Australian dinosaurs scientists discovered. Minmi was named for Minmi Crossing, a crossing in Australia which is where it was discovered. Minmi is a tiny plant-eating dinosaur , walking with four feet. Minmi could have been 10 feet in length, but when as compared to other armored dinosaurs its size is very small. Its back was encased without horns and sharp spikes. There were ridges on the sides of its head, and a few tiny spikes as well. It had a sharp jaw and an enormous flat tooth that was used to crush its food.

7.3. SAUROPELTA

Pronunciation: Sore-oh-pelltah

Meaning of Name Shielded Lizard

Weight 3000 kg

Length 26 feet

Living: North America, Utah, Montana

Time lived: Cretaceous Period (108 million years ago)

Diet: Herbivore

Sauropelta was an armored dinosaur that ate plants. It had four legs as do most armored dinosaurs. However, it had no teeth in the front. It had a beak that resembled one of parrots', and teeth that were hidden behind its mouth.

Sauropelta was a fascinating armor. Its back was covered with bony plates that were used for armor. They weren't part of the skeleton, but were attached to the skin. Bony plates were adorned with sharp horns sticking outwards. The majority of them were located on the neck. It was likely to protect from predators who could move to kill their prey by slicing it on the neck. A few of Sauropelta's bone plates were short-horned, but the majority were just bumps.

8. DINOSAURS WITH HORNS

8.1. TRICERATOPS

How to Pronounce: Try-serra tops

The meaning behind the name is three Horned Head

Weight of 6,000 kg

Size and length: 29.5 feet

Lived: North America, Colorado

Time lived: Late Cretaceous Period (68 million years ago)

Diet: Herbivore

Triceratops is one of the most popular dinosaurs in the world today due to of its head, which appeared to be the shape of a fan. Triceratops was an herbivore, it only ate plants , and was able to walk on four legs. The Triceratops was a horned dinosaur and had two skull horns, each with a large ridge on the side on its skull. The ridge appeared like a curled fan , and could be described as an eagle from a distance. Triceratops was also known as a crown from afar. Triceratops was also equipped with a smaller-sized horn on high up on its nose. It was just as the Rhinoceros is sporting nowadays. It had a beak-shaped mouth similar to a parrot's for eating plants.

8.2. PENTACERATOPS

The Pronunciation to use: Pen-tahserra-tops

The meaning behind the name Meaning of Name: Five Horns

Weight 8000 kg

Height and Length 25 feet

The places where I lived: North America, New Mexico

Time lived: Late Cretaceous Period (76 - 7 millions of years ago)

Diet: Herbivore

Pentaceratops was a resemblance to it was a Triceratops however its head was much larger and also it included an additional horn on both sides of its jaw. Pentaceratops holds the distinction of having the biggest skull among land animals on the planet. Similar to Triceratops, Pentaceratops had a huge skull that was fanned with ridges. However, the skull of Pentaceratops is both longer and larger. It was equipped with three horns similar to Triceratops', and two false horns on both jaws. Pentaceratops made use of these "false" horns to help support the jaw muscles. They were fake horns since they were actually simply bumps.

Pentaceratops also was a parrot-like bird with a beak. consumed only plants, and could even have had a row of teeth in its beak.

9. GIGANT DINOSAURS

9.1. SAUROPOSEIDON

How to Pronounce: Sore-oh-po-teh-sai-don

Meaning of Name The meaning of the name is Earthquake God Lizard

Weight: 50-60 tons

Height 60 feet

Length 100 feet

The places where I lived: Oklahoma, Wyoming, Texas

Time lived: Early Cretaceous Period (40 million years)

Diet: Herbivore

Sauroposeidon Sauroposeidon is the highest living animal that ever lived on the planet. The neck of the animal measured 35 feet in length. It was able to walk with four feet that were hefty and round as an elephant's. The Sauroposeidon included a set of 52 teeth that were shaped like a chisel. It ate

169

and sucked plants up to 1 tonne each day. Its stomach was incredibly powerful in its capacity to digest all that food items.

Researchers have discovered that its stomach could break down rocks and even iron due to its remarkable digestion. It also lived for up to 100 years and was a difficult prey for carnivores.

9.2. BRACHIOSAURUS

What is the correct pronunciation of Brack-ee-uh -sore

Meaning of Name Meaning of Name: Lizard Lizard

Weight 40-80 tons

The height is 40-50 feet.

Length 85 feet

lived: Argentina, parts of South America

Time was lived: Middle to Late Jurassic Period (156-145 million years ago)

Diet: Herbivore

Brachiosaurus was thought to be the tallest dinosaur before it was discovered that Sauroposeidon came to be discovered. As with all sauropods, the Brachiosaurus had four legs and ate plant matter only. It was so heavy that it was unable to walk forwards with ease and, unlike the other sauropods it could not stand up on it's hind legs.

Its teeth were the shape of spoons as well as very large jaw bones. It didn't chew its food , but took the plants in its mouth after slicing the plants off. Contrary to most sauropods Brachiosaurus didn't have an "S" neck like other sauropods. Instead, its neck was pointed upwards diagonally. The shoulders and front legs were bigger than the hind legs and hips which meant that its entire body was pointed upwards diagonally. The tail was also longer and was shorter than the autres sauropod tails.

9.3. GIGANOTOSAURUS

How to Pronounce: Gy-ga-noh-teh-sore-uss

The meaning behind the name: Giant Lizard of the South

Weight 8 tons

Height 23 feet

Length length: 46 feet

lived: Argentina, parts of South America

Time was lived: Late Cretaceous Period (100 - the year 97 million)

Diet: Carnivore

Giganotosaurus is larger than Tyrannosaurus Rex but looked quite similar to it. It had hands that were short, that had only three fingers an almost 6-foot head and a brain as big as the size of a banana. Although the Giganotosaurus had a tiny head, its brain was also a terrifying predator that ate plants and dinosaurs with as large as sauropods and had long necks. Its teeth were 7 inches that were serrated and long as knives. When compared to the T-Rex it was an incredibly large carnivore.

9.4. 9.4. REX

How to Pronounce: Ti/Tie-ra-noh-sore-uss Reks

Meaning of Name The meaning of the name is: Tyrant Lizard King

Weight 7 tons

Height of Between 15 and 20 feet

Length 42 feet

Life in: North America and Mongolia

Time lived: Early Cretaceous Period (67 - 65 millions of years ago)

Diet: Carnivore

Who hasn't heard of the Tyrannosaurus Rex? It had a massive head, very short hands and frightening pointed teeth. It was able to walk on two legs that resembled birds, with three-toed feet, which had horrible claws.

Its legs were powerful , and its feet could reach as high as 3.5 feet in length. It only walked on its feet, but could run up to 15 feet, and could run up to 24 kilometers per hour. People are familiar with the Tyrannosaurus Rex for its small arms. They were about 3 feet long , compared to its five feet long head. This T-Rex is also among the very first massive meat-eating dinosaurs to be discovered.

10. More Dinosaurs...

10.1. COMPSOGNATHUS

How to pronounce: Comp-son-nay-thuss

Meaning of the name The meaning of the name is Pretty Mouth.

Weight 3 kg

The length is 4.5 feet

The people who lived there: Europe; France, Germany

The diet: Herbivore (Fish and Dead Animals)

Compsognathus is among the tiniest dinosaurs that have been discovered. The Compsognathus was a kind of creature of the lizard. It had long tails with a pointed, small head, and a lizard-like nostril. In terms of size, it is similar to today's chicken, and it was equipped with the same type of legs. Its legs were very tall for its size which allowed it to sprint extremely fast, or to catch their food or escape predators. Although that the Compsognathus is a tiny dinosaur, it was one of the plant eaters, but was it was a carnivore. It consumed animals smaller than it and also insects.

10.2. MEGALOSAURUS

How to Pronounce: Meg-ah Low-Sore-Us

The meaning behind the name Great Reptile

Weight 1000 kg

Height 10 feet

Length: 30feet

The time in which I lived: Europe; England

Diet: Carnivore

Megalosaurus was among the first dinosaurs to be discovered in the 16th century, which was around the time of the end of the 16th century. The Megalosaurus also was the first dinosaur to receive an appropriate scientific name, and this was before the term "Dinosaur" was created. The Megalosaurus was very similar to the T-Rex however it had larger arms. It had a neck that was short with a large body, and massive bones. Researchers believe that the Megalosaurus could hunt all sorts of prey and even giant sauropods.

10.3. HESPERONYCHUS

How to Pronounce: Hess-peh-ronn-ih-kuss

The meaning behind the name: Western Claw

Weigh: 1.4 up to 2.3 kg

Length 2 feet

Life: North America; Alberta, Canada

Diet: Insectivore

The time of their lives was during the Cretaceous Period (75 million years ago)

Hesperonychus is known as a theropod meaning it was able to walk on two feet. It was covered with feathers on the body. Also, it had a long tail that was adorned with feathers and was incredibly tiny. The feathers of this bird were vibrant and attractive, particularly the tail. If it resembled any other animal of today It could be mistaken with a peacock that looked strange.

In comparison to the majority of dinosaurs The Hesperonychus is quite tiny. Its size is comparable to squirrels today. Researchers believe that it was higher up in the trees, and could be able to glide from branch to. Though it was able to fly however, it was not able to fly. It was likely an insectivore, and it consumed only insectsas it was a tiny animal and relied on its wings to fly over higher ground. However, it was equipped with tiny steak knife-like teeth, and claws that were similar to the claws of a raptor.

10.4. VELOCIRAPTOR

What to pronounce: Vellos-os-see-rap

Name meaning: Quick Hunter

Weight: 15-30kg

Länge: 5.5 6-foot

Height 3 feet

Lived: Asia; Mongolia, China

The diet: Herbivore (Fish and Dead Animals)

Velociraptor was a reptile species that became famous due to its speed, intelligence, and terrifying set of teeth. The brain of the animal is huge in comparison to its body. It was a meat eater that had tooth-like, sharply curved and sharp teeth that were 2.5 centimeters long. The Velociraptor was a large and flat snout. Its head measured 7 inches in length. The long neck of the animal was shaped like an "s" as well as curved claws on the four of its toes. Scientists have concluded they believe that Velociraptor could be able to run up to 60 kilometers per hour. Its tail was long , but stiff, and was utilized to balance and increase speed when running. Velociraptors were quick, intelligent creatures that were able to divide from their herd and beat heavily armored or horned dinosaurs.

10.5. IGUANODON

The Pronunciation to use: Ig-wa'neh-don

Name Meaning: Iguana Tooth

The weight range is 4-5 tons.

Height between 15 and 20 feet

Length 16 feet

Life in: North America and Mongolia

Diet: Herbivore

It was Iguanadon was a dinosaur that ate plants that was able to walk on the two feet or four. It was toothless, but had a toothy break. It ate with check teeth and ate its food with its fingers. The hands of the animal had 4 fingers, and the thumb spikes ranged from between 2 and 6 inches long and shaped as cones. The feet included three toes, and claws that resembled hooves. Its legs were larger and longer than its arms. It likely utilized its long, flat tail to defend itself. The Iguanadons probably existed in herds. The majority of Iguanadon fossils were discovered together. It was called Iguanadon because its teeth on the cheek were similar to today's Iguana teeth, but with that they were bigger.

10.6. 10.6.

How to Pronounce: Gy-ga-noh-teh-sore-uss

Names Meaning: Roof Lizard or Covered Lizard

Weight: 3,00 kg

Height 9 feet

Length: 26-30 feet

Living: North America, Utah, Wyoming, Colorado and Europe, China, Southern India and Southern Africa

Diet: Herbivore

Stegosaurus is a popular dinosaur due to its back. The back of the dinosaur has an array of large boney, flat, triangular-shaped plates. The triangular plates run along its back and extend to the tail's end. There were 17 plates discovered on its back. The largest was nearly two feet tall and two feet wide.

The Stegosaurus was massively built and even had two tail spikes that were three feet long. The Stegosaurus consumed only soft plants and did not have teeth. Instead, it was equipped with beaks and tiny "cheek" teeth. These teeth were weak and was the reason reasons why the Stegosaurus only consumed soft fruits and vegetables.

11. FUN FACTS!

11.1. BIG DINOSAUR FACTS

The largest dinosaurs stood greater than 50 feet high and greater than 100 feet. It's the Sauroposeidon.

The biggest dinosaurs that have ever lived are plant-eaters. Herbivores.

* The largest dinosaur to date has been the Brachiosaurus. Its weight could be as high as 80 tonnes that is the same weight as 17 African elephants. It's also the biggest dinosaur that has been discovered in the museum. The largest skeleton that was found was 16 meters high and extended to 26 meters.

* The longest tooth of a dinosaur that ate meat is the Tyrannosaurus Rex. It is approximately 8 inches wide.

* Hesperonychus is the world's smallest dinosaur that eats meat. It's only 19 inches in height and one Meter long. It's the same size as an typical chicken.

11.2. SCIENTIFIC DINOSAUR FACTS

* The term "Dinosaur" is a Greek word"dinosaur", which is a reference to "Terrible Lizard". Richard Owen, and English paleontologist in 1842 , used the word to describe huge size of the dinosaurs. Many believed that it was due to the terrifying look of the dinosaurs, that the word was chosen in this way.

* Megalosaurus was the first dinosaur officially identified and was first named in 1824, when it was discovered by William Buckland.

* Someone that studies dinosaurs can be referred to as an Paleontologist.

* When the people of China first discovered dinosaur bones, they believed that they were bones of huge dragons.

* There are over 900 dinosaurs discovered by scientists in the present, and many there are many more being discovered, but they do not have names that are appropriate yet.

11.3. SMART DINOSAUR FACTS

The most stupid reptile is Stegosaurus. The Stegosaurus's body of two tons and incredible spiked back are terrifying, however its brain, which is the size of a walnut, isn't. It was not particularly smart due to its brain size.

* Scientists can determine the intelligence of a dinosaur by the size of their body is as well as the size of their brain. Some dinosaurs such as the Stegosaurus have massive bodies, but brains that are extremely small. Some dinosaurs have medium-sized bodies, but brains as big as an apple that makes them more intelligent that the Stegosaurus.

Conclusion

Dinosaurs are a popular subject even though they're extinct. Their incredible appearance and mysterious way they died and lived have inspired films and books. The dinosaurs were amazing terrifying creatures that lived in a time where the natural world was abundant with fruit, plants, animals as well as water and vegetation.

Discovering dinosaurs provided us to see how the world used be many millions of years ago, long before humans were even a thing. It's exciting and enlightening to know about these amazing creatures who once ruled the planet.

Dinosaurs, as with all animals , today come in a variety of varieties. Some are huge, others are small , and there are some that can fly, swim, and glide. They hunted, were hunted, and survived as any other animal. They're really fascinating and are similar to the modern animals with the exception that they were bigger, tougher and had sharper teeth as well as claws.

www.ingramcontent.com/pod-product-compliance
Lightning Source LLC
Chambersburg PA
CBHW062116040426
42336CB00041B/1243